M & E HANDBOOKS

M & E Handbooks are recommended reading for examination syllabuses all over the world. Because each Handbook covers its subject clearly and concisely books in the series form a vital part of many college, university, school and home study courses.

Handbooks contain detailed information stripped of unnecessary padding, making each title a comprehensive self-tuition course. They are amplified with numerous self-testing questions in the form of Progress Tests at the end of each chapter, each text-referenced for easy checking. Every Handbook closes with an appendix which advises on examination technique. For all these reasons, Handbooks are ideal for pre-examination revision.

The handy pocket-book size and competitive price make Handbooks the perfect choice for anyone who wants to grasp the essentials of a subject quickly and easily.

THE M & E HANDBOOK SERIES

Marketing Research

Tony Proctor
MA, MPhil, MBIM, FRSA
Head of Department of Business and Management Studies, Bolton Institute of Technology

and

Marilyn A. Stone
BSc(Econ), H.N.D. (Business Studies), Dip Inst M, MIMRA
Department of Business Organisation
Heriot-Watt University, Edinburgh

MACDONALD AND EVANS

Macdonald & Evans Ltd
Estover, Plymouth PL6 7PZ

First published 1978
Reprinted (with amendments) 1982

7121 1291 X

Printed in Great Britain by
Hazell Watson & Viney Ltd,
Aylesbury, Bucks

Preface

The efficient management of an enterprise demands that executives are able to cope with the uncertainties which are forced upon a company by its environment. Environmental "threats" may arise in many ways and from different sources. A company may actively choose to enter new markets or to develop new products. Alternatively, new competition in a traditional market may cause the company to lose some of its share of the total market sales. In either situation, competitive pressure or new environments, it is the role of marketing research to investigate the complex problems associated with marketing under unfamiliar, as well as known, conditions.

Traditionally, manufacturers of fast-moving consumer goods have led the way in formal marketing research. The larger producers of industrial products and consumer durables are also developing their expertise in the knowledge that efficient marketing research is an essential prerequisite to successful marketing. Similarly, there is a growing awareness amongst the smaller firms that they too can benefit from the use of marketing research. They may not have the resources or the desire to mount studies on the scale of their larger competitors but they are aware of the benefits of relevant marketing research work.

Industry's growing appreciation of the value of marketing research has created a demand for courses to provide students with a fundamental knowledge of what marketing research is, and its practical applications to business. In this HANDBOOK the major aspects of the subject are discussed and illustrated. Our aim is to give the student a concise guide in a form that is both simple to understand and stimulating to study. To gain this end we have attempted to temper the more academic aspects with examples and advice drawn from our own considerable industrial experience. Although the undergraduate market has been our primary target, we hope that this HANDBOOK will reach a wider readership and that it will become a valuable source-book in many sectors of industry. The book will be particularly useful to D.M.S., BEC, H.N.D. (Business Studies), Institute of Marketing Diploma, M.R.S. Diploma students and undergraduate courses.

The compilation of the book has been essentially a joint exercise but our specialities vary. Thus, one of us (T.P.) has been responsible for Chapters I–IV, IX and XII, whilst the other (M.A.S.) has contributed Chapters V–VII, X and XI.

The authors gratefully acknowledge the permission of Heriot-Watt and Strathclyde Universities to reproduce questions from recent B.A. degree examination papers in Appendix X. In addition the authors are grateful to the Institute of Marketing for permission to include questions from recent Diploma examinations in the same Appendix.

August, 1978

T.P.
M.A.S.

Contents

PART ONE
MARKETING RESEARCH AND DECISION MAKING

CHAPTER I
Introduction to Marketing Research

1. Introduction. In this chapter marketing research is defined and some of the marketing problems that it can help to resolve are mentioned. Since the type of research is decision orientated, attention is next focused on the role of information in decision making and the concept of expected pay-off as a criterion of choice. Marketing decisions can at best only be made under conditions of partial uncertainty. The information needed by an organisation to help resolve uncertainty can be both financially expensive and time consuming to obtain. The chapter concludes by examining the idea that there is a need to take account of the costs and benefits of collecting different types of information, which are relevant to the marketing decision at hand.

2. What is marketing research? Marketing research is a formalised means of obtaining information to be used in making marketing decisions. Effective marketing decisions are based on sound information and relate to the pricing, distribution, promotion and product specification of a firm's goods or services. Such decisions might be:

(*a*) whether a new product should be introduced at a particular time;
(*b*) whether the product range should encompass more than one model;
(*c*) what retail prices should be suggested for the product;
(*d*) what discounts should be allowed to dealers;
(*e*) through what channels of distribution the product should be marketed;

(*f*) what advertising budget is recommended for the introductory period;

(*g*) in what media and in what amounts the advertising budget should be allocated.

Marketing research can be divided into three activities:

(*a*) *Exploratory research*, concerned with discovering the general form of the decision or problem situation.

(*b*) *Descriptive research*, focusing on the accurate description of the variables in the decision or problem situation.

(*c*) *Causal research*, specifying the nature of the functional relationship between two or more variables in the problem situation.

3. The importance of marketing research. In decision-making the costs and benefits, which may result from pursuing a line of action, have to be considered. Frequently these costs and benefits can be quantified readily. This makes it easier to make an objective decision.

Many marketing decisions are made on the basis of hunches or trial and error reasoning. Whilst in the past such reasoning has led to successful decisions being implemented, commonly it has resulted in costly failures. The significance of marketing research has been appreciated for some years now, but its adoption as a fully developed and formalised function within the firm is not yet widespread.

RESEARCH FOR MARKETING DECISIONS

4. Types of decisions. A decision situation is one in which choice is exercised amongst a number of options. Decisions can be placed into three categories:

(*a*) *Operational*—which govern the mechanical aspects of performing a task.

(*b*) *Administrative*—which facilitate the co-ordination of various tasks and operational decisions.

(*c*) *Strategic*—which concern the purpose for which tasks are undertaken.

EXAMPLE: A firm manufactures and markets boots and shoes. In order that goods be delivered to the retail outlets, they have to be physically transported from the firm's warehouse to the chosen destinations. Operational decisions govern deployment of warehousemen and drivers, choice of loading and unloading gear, method of packing, route selection etc. Administrative decisions involve co-ordination of all these activities so that the task can be well performed. Strategic decisions relate to the choice of destinations—that is, which retailers ought to be selected for the distribution of shoes in order to achieve product availability to customers.

Marketing research is predominantly concerned with strategic decisions.

5. Marketing strategy. Strategy involves planning for the accomplishment of an objective. The two key elements are:

(*a*) the plan; and
(*b*) the objective.

Returning to the example in **4** above, the objective of a distribution system is to achieve product availability to customers, affording maximum satisfaction to the customer at a reasonable cost to the firm. In other words, the aim is to achieve the greatest possible contentment to allow a reasonable level of profit for the firm. The task of the firm is to choose a group of distributors which will enable this aim or objective to be achieved satisfactorily. The planning aspect involves operational, administrative and strategic decisions.

6. Decision making under conditions of uncertainty. Strategic decisions are effectively choices made by the firm which involve organisations, individuals and events which are outside the sphere of its direct control. Such decisions can be:

(*a*) *Pricing decisions.* What price to charge customers and/or middlemen?

(*b*) *Product decisions.* What type, range, combination, variation, quality or design of products to offer customers?

(*c*) *Promotion decisions.* What type, combination or variation of advertising, personal selling and sales promotion to choose?

(*d*) *Distribution decisions.* Which channels of distribution should be used? What method of physical distribution should be adopted?

EXAMPLE: A firm appoints a distributor but cannot be certain that this choice will lead to a greater sales achievement than if another distributor were used. The act of appointing a distributor means that the firm loses some control over the marketing of the product to the ultimate consumer.

Since the above is always inevitable, the best that a firm can try to do is to dispel some of the uncertainty surrounding such a decision. If a firm has perfect information beforehand about the outcome of a line of action ensuing from a specific choice situation, then there is no uncertainty in the decision situation. To resolve the uncertainty, information is required. Moreover, the better or more perfect the information, the less uncertainty there will be when the eventual decision is taken.

Information has two important dimensions: quality and quantity. Whilst it is extremely advantageous to have as high a quality of information as possible, too much information can be disadvantageous. Men and machines have only limited information processing capacity. It follows that if too much information is presented "information" overload can occur and the system, human or mechanical, may break down. Achieving the correct equilibrium in terms of quantity and quality of information is critical to good decision making. It is the task of the marketing researcher to achieve this balance, within the financial and time constraints imposed upon his or her work.

7. Choice criterion models. Strategic decisions necessitate choice amongst a variety of options. Choice of option will depend on how well the selected option matches with the choice criteria. Every option will have a pay-off or benefit to the decision maker —in addition it will also have a cost. The relative pay-offs, or benefits of individual options and their associated costs have to be matched with the choice criteria. If two options have different pay-offs and the same costs then, other things being equal, the option with the higher pay-off should be selected. If two options have the same pay-off and the same cost, the degree of certainty in the two possible outcomes should be considered.

EXAMPLE: A firm may be considering the introduction of three new product ideas, but unfortunately it only has the resources to develop one of them. It is assumed that all products will incur the same costs. Two estimates of sales potential are prepared:

Product	*Optimistic level of sales predicted*	*Pessimistic level of sales predicted*
	£ m. p.a.	£ m. p.a.
A	4.0	2.0
B	4.0	1.5
C	3.0	2.5

Optimistic level—the best that can be expected.
Pessimistic level—the worst that can be anticipated.

The selection, if any, of an idea for development depends on the firm's choice criterion model. The model will reflect the firm's risk taking propensity and level of aspiration. Briefly there are several models that the firm can adopt and three of these are discussed below.

(*a*) *Maxi-max.* To select the course of action with the maximum possible pay-off. In the example above, both A and B have the best possible pay-off at £4 million per annum. A decision-maker adopting this decision model would be unable therefore to differentiate between the projects. He might well decide by the toss of a coin.

(*b*) *Mini-max.* To adopt the course of action which will minimise the maximum loss. In the example, option C best satisfies this criterion. The minimum (pessimistic) sales expected is £2.5 million per annum.

(*c*) *Expected pay-off.* To select the course of action which promises the best average pay-off. In the example above, the expected average pay-offs are found by adding together the pessimistic and optimistic levels of sales predicted and dividing the sum by two. This gives an expected average pay-off to each of the products as follows:

Product	A	£3.0 million
	B	£2.75 million
	C	£2.75 million

The best average pay-off is that of product A. Suppose the table in the example above is rewritten as follows:

Product	*Optimistic level of sales predicted (probability of occurrence:* 0.4)	*Pessimistic level of sales predicted (probability of occurrence:* 0.6)
	£ m. p.a.	£ m. p.a.
A	4.0	2.0
B	4.0	1.5
C	3.0	2.5

It is estimated that there is a probability of 0.4 (a 40 per cent chance) that sales will reach the optimistic level and a probability of 0.6 (a 60 per cent chance) that sales will only reach the pessimistic level (the probabilities always sum to unity). The expected pay-offs are calculated:

Product	(*Optimistic estimate × Probability of occurrence*)	+	(*Pessimistic estimate × Probability of occurrence*)	=	*Expected pay off* £ m. p.a.
A	4.0×0.4	+	2.0×0.6	=	2.8
B	4.0×0.4	+	1.5×0.6	=	2.5
C	3.0×0.4	+	2.5×0.6	=	2.7

In this illustration product A has the best expected pay-off. If the firm applies mini-max or maxi-max rules to this problem it will act as in (*a*) and (*b*) above as follows.

(*a*) *Maxi-max.* It might prefer A to C, since the former offers a better "optimistic level of sales" (£4 million versus £3 million).

(*b*) *Mini-max.* It might prefer C to A, since the former offers a better "pessimistic level of sale" (£2.5 million versus £2 million).

Obviously the firm may choose not to develop any of the products, depending on its level of aspiration. If, for instance, the firm expects a new product to generate at least £3 million per annum, then unless it uses a maxi-max choice criterion model, it will reject all the products.

THE VALUE OF MARKETING RESEARCH

8. The cost and value of information. Good information is clearly essential for the making of consistently effective decisions, but information can be expensive to obtain. The question to be answered is "how much time and money ought to be spent to facilitate effective decision making?"

The decision problem of how much to spend on marketing research must eventually be quantified. The cost of research will range from zero (no research) to whatever amount is necessary to design and execute the study. A quantitative evaluation of the net value of the information collected is the ideal basis for the decision to use or not use marketing research.

9. Cost–benefit analysis. Cost–benefit analysis was developed in response to the need to evaluate alternative projects without there being a profit criterion. Essentially, it is a system for identifying which decision option will maximise benefits or minimise costs, or, maximise the cost to benefit ratio.

Benefits and costs can be expressed in non-monetary terms, such as the number of respondents interviewed, the number of qualified prospects identified, the number of media evaluated etc.

The following steps are involved:

(*a*) Review the marketing objectives of the decision maker.

(*b*) Define the objectives of the research.

(*c*) Define the benefits that are to be used as evaluative criteria.

(*d*) State the purpose of the study—to maximise the benefits, minimise the costs etc.

(*e*) Specify the research alternatives.

(*f*) Provide for the inclusion of risk in the analysis by assigning probabilities to the possible outcomes (expressed as pay-off benefits) of each alternative.

(*g*) Calculate the expected values for the benefits of each option.

10. Illustration of the application of cost-benefit analysis. The following numerical illustration shows how the above steps are put into practice:

Purpose of the investigation:

(*a*) To obtain product positioning for a new product.

(*b*) To establish consumer attitudes towards a new product.

(*c*) To ascertain the number of usable survey responses.

(*d*) To maximise the ratio of benefits to cost, subject to a minimum of 500 usable survey responses and a maximum cost of £10 000.

(*e*) To establish research alternatives.

Alternative	*Benefits*	*Cost*
R 1—mail	600–1000 usable responses	£8000
R 2—telephone	400– 700 usable responses	£5000
R 3—personal	700– 900 usable responses	£8000

(*f*)

Research alternative	*Pay-offs: responses (benefits and possible outcomes (probability of occurrence shown in brackets))*		
	S 1	S 2	S 3
R 1	600 (0.2)	800 (0.4)	1000 (0.4)
R 2	400 (0.4)	500 (0.4)	700 (0.2)
R 3	700 (0.5)	800 (0.3)	900 (0.2)

(*g*) Decision values.

Expected value of the benefit (responses)	*Cost*	*Benefit to cost ratio*
R 1: $600 \times 0.2 + 800 \times 0.4 + 1000 \times 0.4 = \underline{840}$	£8000	0.105: 1
R 2: $400 \times 0.4 + 500 \times 0.4 + 700 \times 0.2 = \underline{500}$	£5000	0.100: 1
R 3: $700 \times 0.5 + 800 \times 0.3 + 900 \times 0.2 = \underline{770}$	£8000	0.096: 1

Research alternative R 1 offers the best benefit to cost ratio and meets the two constraints.

11. Summary. The chapter introduces the idea that marketing research is an aid to marketing decision making. The nature of marketing decisions is explored in some depth as is the method of exercising choice between different options. The concept of expected pay-off or benefit as the basic criterion of decisions is suggested and the role of research as the provider of the necessary quantitative estimates noted. The chapter also points out that marketing research not only has the task of providing quantitative data, but also must obtain qualitative data in addition. Marketing research's task is not only to provide data but it has to be instrumental in helping to define problems and to suggest solutions.

PROGRESS TEST 1

1. Suggest the costs and benefits that might accrue to a firm in each of the following instances:
   (*a*) The introduction of a new product.
   (*b*) An advertisement.
   (*c*) A market research study. (7)
2. The table below shows the pay–offs or benefits associated with six strategic options:

Option	*Lowest pay–off* £	*Probability of occurrence*	*Highest pay–off* £	*Probability of occurrence*
1	250 000	0.65	436 000	0.35
2	238 000	0.55	512 000	0.45
3	246 000	0.50	488 000	0.50
4	228 000	0.75	427 000	0.25
5	219 000	0.70	450 000	0.30
6	261 000	0.55	471 000	0.45

State which option you would choose to adopt, assuming:
   (*a*) mini-max criterion;
   (*b*) maxi-max criterion;
   (*c*) expected pay-off criterion.

What impact would the constraint that an option must promise a return of at least £370 000 have on your decision? (7)

3. A marketing research manager must decide between the following six research designs, selecting the one which offers the best benefit to cost ratio. Which one would you recommend, bearing in mind that the minimum acceptable sample size is 2200 responses and the cost must not exceed £2400?

Option	*Low estimate*	*Probability*	*High estimate*	*Probability*	*Cost £*
1	1000	0.5	2600	0.5	2150
2	1750	0.6	2850	0.4	2175
3	1950	0.4	2500	0.6	2850
4	2200	0.8	2750	0.2	2450
5	2000	0.9	2600	0.1	2300
6	1500	0.5	3000	0.5	2250

(10)

CHAPTER II

Problem Definition and Research Design

1. Introduction. In this chapter some of the types of marketing problems which can arise are considered, as are the ways in which marketing research can help them to be solved. An example is shown of how a problem situation can be modelled so as to facilitate the logical achievement of a solution. The chapter proceeds by examining the development of a research design. Research design, methodology and applications are discussed, as are the types of errors that can arise. The final section illustrates how a research design should be incorporated into a research proposal.

PROBLEMS AND MODELS

2. Types of marketing problems. Marketing problems typically involve strategic decisions. Three such examples are:

(*a*) Should the firm decide to introduce a new product or brand?
(*b*) How effective has a particular advertising programme been in terms of creating sales?
(*c*) Where should distribution depots be sited and how many should there be?

3. A new product introduction decision. In relation to a decision concerning the introduction of a new product a number of measurements, or criteria, have to be developed against which to evaluate the product, product idea or concept. The criteria used have to reflect the particular objectives that the firm is pursuing. If the product is assumed to be "a new brand" and it can be presumed that the firm has all the necessary resources to develop and launch such a product, then the final decisions will depend on the incremental sales and/or profits that this new brand could generate. Emphasis here is on the word "incremental" since the actual sales or profits generated by the product may not represent the true worth of the product. Profit and/or sales interaction with the other brands marketed by the firm may occur and it may have the effect of increasing sales of a complementary product or decreasing sales of a similar brand.

Not only must the introduction of a new product have an overall incremental effect upon sales and profits, but it must also meet certain financial requirements stipulated by the firm. The firm may require that the brand generates a certain return on investment or will generate sufficient revenues to achieve break-even in a specific time period. A solution to this problem requires forecasts to be made of incremental profits and sales.

4. Advertising effectiveness. While the problem of measuring advertising effectiveness affects most companies, it is not easy to solve. The problem has two complicating factors:

(*a*) An advertisement does not necessarily create a sale, yet it may still perform a useful function.

(*b*) An advertisement may create a sale after the lapse of a considerable length of time.

The two factors are related. An advertisement carries a message or information about a product or service; it attracts attention, provokes interest or even desire to purchase the product, but it may not necessarily result in action being taken to purchase the product.

Customers pass through several stages prior to making a purchase. The function of advertising may simply be to move the potential customer from an early stage to a later one.

EXAMPLE: Five stages are proposed in the consumer adoption of a new product process: (1) awareness; (2) interest; (3) evaluation; (4) trial; and (5) adoption.

If it is assumed that a consumer durable purchase is being considered, it will be seen that a sale is only generated at stage (5) adoption. Nevertheless, advertisements must be specifically designed to move consumers through each of these stages. Measuring advertising effectiveness requires a different approach according to the purpose of the advertisements. Where a specific programme is designed to create brand awareness, then the measures taken should reflect consumer recollections of the advertised brand and the advertisements.

In this instance, the problem is complicated by the fact that advertising fulfills a number of functions during the pre-purchase activity stages. Any attempt to measure the effectiveness of advertising in creating sales must take these factors into account.

5. Depot siting. This problem involves selecting a combination of warehouses, strategically situated in an area, such that they enable the firm to optimise its level of customer service in relationship to distribution costs. A firm seeks to minimise its distribution costs, thereby either retaining any savings in increased profits or passing on the savings to the customer in terms of lower prices. This aspect of the problem calls for the firm to determine what is the optimum number of warehouses to maintain, how large they should be and where they should be sited. To resolve the problem the firm has to conduct a cost-benefit analysis to determine the amount of centralisation which most suits its own distribution system. More regional warehouses may enable the firm to give a better level of customer service but it may also add substantially to distribution costs. Such a problem requires an estimate of the incremental sales and profits attributable in each instance to the provision of each additional warehouse.

6. Modelling the decision situation—introducing a new brand. In modelling any decision situation, the following must be considered:

(*a*) The set of decision rules that should be adopted to govern how management choice is made.

(*b*) The flow directions of information required to enable decision rules to be applied.

(*c*) The sources of information and the method in which they are to be acquired.

EXAMPLE: Introducing a new brand. A firm has the following criteria for decision making:

(*a*) *Decision rule.* The decision to launch the product nationally is based upon the probability that the product has an 80 per cent chance of achieving £1 million sales per annum at the retail level and a certain percentage return on investment.

(*b*) *Flows of information.* Estimates of annual sales volume in monetary terms are required together with estimates of investment, marketing and production costs.

(*c*) *Sources of information.* Sales estimates are to be obtained from experimental test-markets held in London, Birmingham and Glasgow. The various internal departments of the firm are to provide estimates of costs.

From the above, the model shown in Fig. 1 can be constructed.

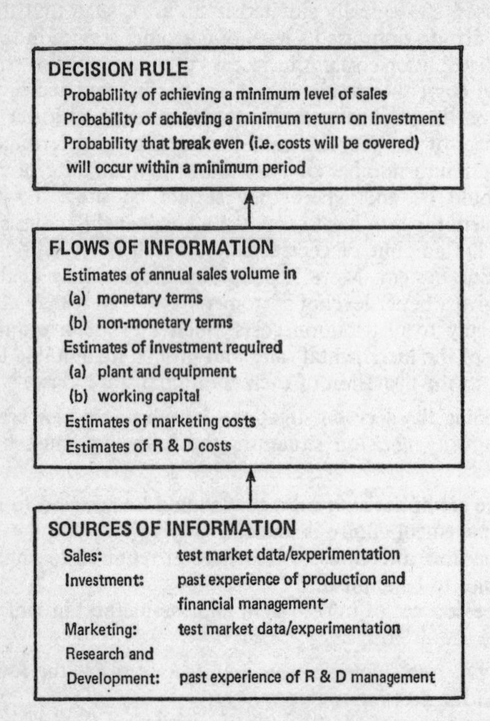

FIG. 1 *Decision rules, flows of information and sources of information—new product decisions.*

7. An illustration of a new product decision. A firm estimates on the basis of an experimental test market, that there is a high chance that sales of £800 000 at the retail level can be achieved for a new product in the first year of operation. In addition at least £1 000 000 per annum in sales can be expected in each of the next five years. Thereafter, it is felt that the product will be superseded by a new product. The firm recognises that the product will require an initial investment of £900 000 and that research and development and marketing costs will amount to £1 000 000 initially. Marketing costs are estimated to be approximately £300 000 per annum thereafter (during years 1–6 inclusive). Product profitability is expected to run at the rate of 20 per cent of sales.

The firm operates a single decision rule: that each new product must generate a return on investment of at least 15 per cent over the life of the product.

Calculation of the return on investment (R.O.I.) that the new product will generate.

Year	*Investment* (£)	*Expenditure on R. & D. advertising* (£)	*Revenue* (£)	*15% Discount factor*
0	900 000	700 000	—	1.000
1	—	300 000	800 000	0.870
2	—	300 000	1 000 000	0.756
3	—	300 000	1 000 000	0.657
4	—	300 000	1 000 000	0.571
5	—	300 000	1 000 000	0.497
6	—	300 000	1 000 000	0.432

Discounted cash flow (£)

Out	*In*	*Difference ("In" minus "Out")*
1 600 000	—	−1 600 000
261 000	696 000	435 000
226 800	756 000	529 200
197 100	657 000	459 900
171 300	571 000	399 700
149 100	497 000	347 900
		+ 571 700

NOTE: The discounted cash flows both "Out" and "In" are obtained by multiplying the respective expenditure and revenue columns by the appropriate discount factor.

e.g.

Year 3 (Out): $300\,000 \times 0.657 = 197\,100$

It will be seen that the total difference ("In" minus "Out") is positive. This shows that the product is likely to generate an R.O.I. of at least 15 per cent. If this figure had been negative then the converse would have been true. Different discount factor values can be obtained from tables (*see* Appendix VI) and the same procedure is adopted as above, depending upon the R.O.I. that is stipulated in the decision criteria.

In the example given, the firm would be justified in launching the product.

RESEARCH DESIGN AND RESEARCH OBJECTIVES

8. The nature of research design. Research design is the plan, structure and strategy of investigation conceived so as to obtain answers to research questions. The plan is the over-all scheme of the research and contains an outline of what the researcher proposes to do. The structure of the research is the outline, scheme or model of how the variables are interrelated. In drawing diagrams that outline the variables and their juxtapositions, structural schemes are built for accomplishing operational research purposes. Strategy implies how the research objectives will be attained and how the problems encountered in the research will be tackled.

Research designs are evolved to enable the researcher to answer questions objectively, accurately and economically. The design states what observations to make, how to make them and how to analyse the quantitative representations of the observations.

9. Design techniques. Whilst the design itself may specify the use of rigorous techniques, it also calls for considerable imagination and ingenuity. It is very seldom that two independent researchers would propose the same design in detail. There is no single textbook approach to research design, but there are several tasks to be performed in proposing a project design and which can help in the selection of an appropriate design.

(*a*) *Definition of the problem.* Whilst it is the recognition of a problem that usually instigates research in the first instance, the problem must be clearly stated to facilitate the research design stage. For example, a decline in company sales may raise the idea that marketing research should be undertaken to ascertain the cause of the sales drop and to recommend the action that should be implemented. The problem needs to be stated more precisely, however, which may necessitate undertaking preliminary research to ascertain how widespread the sales fall has been through the firm's product range.

(*b*) *Specifying what information is required to make a decision.* It is important for the executive and the researcher to work very closely together. They should jointly identify problems and solutions. Since it is the role of the executive to make decisions, he must indicate precisely what kinds of information will be required and the format in which such information should be presented. If the decision concerns the introduction of a new product, the executive must specify how confident he needs to be that a given level of sales will be achieved.

(*c*) *Identifying data sources and the cost of extracting data.* The quantity and quality of the information provided by the research cannot be any better than the data sources from which it is drawn, which in turn affects the quality of the decision. However, it should be remembered that the cost of extracting information must not exceed the value of the information to the decision-maker.

(*d*) *Data sources and methodology selection.* The cost and the effect of the technique chosen, together with the data used, must be balanced against the value of, and the need for, the information they will provide. Time is also a factor which needs to be closely controlled.

(*e*) *Selecting resources.* Personnel and material resources must be chosen, their availability confirmed and their costs estimated.

(*f*) *Preparing a formal plan of action.* A formal plan of action entails a statement of *what* is to be attempted, *how* it is to be implemented, *when* it will be done, *who* is to do it, and the costs envisaged.

10. An illustration of a research design incorporated in research proposal. A proposal for a study of the U.K. small car market.

I OBJECTIVES

1. Describe the under 1300 c.c. car market in the U.K.

(*a*) Determine its size—the number of units sold and the monetary value.

(*b*) Determine the geographical distribution of unit sales.

(*c*) Determine product features and their distribution by retail price.

(*d*) Determine the distribution of prices.

(*e*) Determine the proportion of new car sales involving "trade-ins".

2. Determine a personal profile of buyers: include the following characteristics:

(*a*) age;
(*b*) family status;
(*c*) occupation;
(*d*) income;
(*e*) family size.

3. Determine the distribution of the following factors involved in sales:

(*a*) the number of dealers visited before a purchase is completed;

(*b*) the time between the first visit and the actual purchase;

(*c*) retail or dealer demonstrations during the shopping period.

4. Determine the order of motivating influences affecting the choice of brand.

II METHODOLOGY

1. Obtain the following details from the client:

(*a*) a list of car brands to be included in the study;
(*b*) a list of car manufacturers;
(*c*) a list of its own dealers.

2. Visit publishers of car trade journals.

3. Visit motor car shows and exhibitions (where appropriate) to supplement information.

4. Execute a randomised survey of small car owners.

(*a*) Pick out newly registered cars at random and attach a mail questionnaire to the windscreen (under the wipers).

(*b*) Use a mail questionnaire to extract information.

(*c*) Conduct a pilot study of 30 car owners beforehand.

(*d*) Distribute 2000 questionnaires.

5. Analyse the data and summarise it in tabular or graphical form.

6. Correlate the survey data with economic and demographic data for the regional markets, using linear regression analysis.
7. Collect literature from manufacturers and summarise the data.
8. Prepare a formal written report and give the client a personal briefing.

III SCHEDULE AND PRICE

1. The study will be completed within 120 days on receipt of instructions.
2. The price is £*X* plus direct expenses. Expenses will not exceed £*X* and will be fully documented.

11. Summary. Three types of marketing problems have been discussed:

(*a*) a new product decision;
(*b*) measuring advertising effectiveness;
(*c*) determining where distribution depots should be sited and how many there should be in total.

The new product decision problem was then examined in detail and a quantitative example given to illustrate how such a decision might be taken. The example was overly simplified but readers interested in this topic should consult the texts relating to "New products" mentioned in the Bibliography. Decision rules, flows of information and information sources were highlighted as the important elements of any descriptive model of a problem situation.

The next section concerned research design and research objectives. The important tasks needing to be performed to assist in the selection of an appropriate research design were enumerated. The final section was used to illustrate a research design incorporated in a research proposal.

PROGRESS TEST 2

1. List as many marketing problems as you can. How many of these problems involve "incremental" sales and/or profits? **(2, 3)**
2. Suggest:

(*a*) decision rules;

(*b*) flows of information;
(*c*) sources of information;

as they are relevant to the measuring of the effectiveness of an advertising campaign aimed at creating "awareness" of a new product. **(4, 6)**

3. Draw up a research proposal, incorporating a research design for a study of the "pleasure cruiser" market. **(10)**

PART TWO

SCIENTIFIC FOUNDATION OF MARKETING RESEARCH

CHAPTER III

A Quantitative Basis for Research

1. Introduction. This chapter presents those basic statistical and mathematical methods and techniques which are necessary for an understanding of marketing research methodology.

In the first section the need for statistics in research is examined, paying particular attention to the role of statistics as an estimator which enables marketing decisions to be taken on the basis of objective information.

In the remaining sections particular attention is paid to statistical estimation and there is an introduction to statistical tests of significance.

2. The need for statistics in marketing research. Marketing research is conducted to uncover information vital to the solution of a practical problem. The researcher, regardless of his speciality ought to be able to interpret the statistical content of applied and theoretical research, and must be fully conversant with the application of the same techniques. This requires that he knows the meaning of statistical terms and is familiar with attributes and applications of each method.

Marketing researchers assess many different types of data. Much of the data is amassed from surveys and experimentation, other is from past experience and historical data, for example, from past sales records. A knowledge of the methods of statistics aids in the correct analysis and interpretation of sometimes considerable data.

The following illustrates the kind of information that can be obtained from analysis of data. From a set of data portraying, for instance, sales of automatic washing machines in the U.K. over a given period and a set of data portraying economic and demographic trends and the state of the company's marketing effort over the same period, the following types of analysis can be made.

(*a*) Averages can be calculated. They give a picture of the typical performance of the objective of the study.

(*b*) The variability of the measurements can be determined. By using averages as a point of reference the spread of scores or observations about the central point can be determined.

(*c*) Graphs, tables and figures can be prepared to portray clearly the nature of the objective of the study.

(*d*) The relationship that one variable has with another can be established. For example, it might be of interest to find the relationship between economic climate and total market sales; between advertising and market share; or between floor space given to the display of a product and achieved sales. The statistics in these instances are termed "correlation coefficients".

(*e*) One set of variables or a combination of variables can be used to predict future sales behaviour.

(*f*) The performance of one promotional method can be compared with that made by another and the significance of any differences can be tested. For example, suppose that an electricity showroom is testing a new special discount offer on a range of washing machines. Two situations are envisaged:

(*i*) a discount is offered on automatics;

(*ii*) a similar discount is offered on non-automatics.

The two deals are offered independently for two separate six-week periods. That is, a discount is offered on automatics only in the first six-week period and on non-automatics only during the second six-week period. By inspection of the sales figures it can be ascertained whether or not the sales in the two periods differ significantly from one another. Such an experiment might give an indication of whether discounts are more effective on non-automatics than on automatics, as a means of promoting sales (*see* IX for a more detailed discussion on this kind of problem).

(*g*) Inferences can be drawn about a large population by taking measurements of a sample drawn from that population. The drawing of statistical inferences should be one of the chief activities of marketing research.

The drawing of inferences, the making of predictions and the testing of significances are all examples of inferential statistics. Averages, graphs and measures of dispersion are all examples of descriptive statistics.

3. Averages. The three common averages are the arithmetic mean, the median and the mode. When someone refers to an "average" figure it is important to know to what kind of average reference is being made. As will be seen below the mean, median and mode can have different values and in some cases the difference between them can be quite considerable. By referring to one kind of "average" rather than another it is quite possible to give a totally different picture than would have been the case had another "average" been used. The arithmetic mean is the most commonly used "average" in practice though in every-day speech, "average" often refers to the modal value.

(*a*) *Arithmetic mean.* This is equal to the sum of the values of all the observations divided by the number of observations (or cases). The sample mean and the population mean must be distinguished from one another. If all the elements in the "population" are observed the arithmetic mean is called the "population mean", otherwise it is a "sample mean". The population mean is defined by the formula:

$$\mu = \frac{\Sigma X}{N}$$

where μ = the population mean;

Σ = the sum of all values of the . . . element;
X = the value of each element observed or each case;
N = the number of cases or observations.

In the case of the sample mean the formula is:

$$\bar{X} = \frac{\Sigma X}{n}$$

where $\bar{X}$ = the sample mean;
n = the size of the sample.

(*b*) *The median.* This is the middle value of all the observations arrayed in order of magnitude.

(*c*) *The mode.* This is the value in a distribution which occurs most frequently.

EXAMPLE: For the following distribution of numbers find the

arithmetic mean, the median and the mode. Distribution of numbers is 2, 3, 3, 5, 7, 7, 9, 8, 4, 8, 2, 8.

Arithmetic mean = 5.5
The median = 6.0 (half way between 5 and 7)
The mode = 8.0

4. Dispersion. The spread of observed values in a distribution is referred to as "dispersion". The most common measures of dispersion are the range, the variance and the standard deviation of the data.

(*a*) *The range.* This is the difference between the highest and the lowest of an array of numbers. In the example in **3** above the range is:

$$9-2=7$$

(*b*) *The variance.* This is the "average" of the squares of the deviations from the mean (i.e. the difference between an observed value and the mean, all squared). Population variance is defined by the formula:

$$\sigma^2 = \frac{\Sigma(X-\mu)^2}{N}$$

where σ^2 = the population variance and X, μ and N are as before.

The variance of a sample is defined by the formula:

$$s^2 = \frac{\Sigma(X-\bar{X})^2}{n}$$

where s^2 is the variance of the sample.

In the example in **3** above the variance is

$$\frac{75}{11} = 6.82$$

NOTE: In the case of small samples (n = 30 or less) the value n is replaced by $(n-1)$ for calculation of the variance.

(*c*) *The standard deviation.* This is the square root of the variance. It is mathematically defined as:

$$\sigma = (\sigma^2)^{\frac{1}{2}} \quad \text{(population)}$$

or

$$s = (s^2)^{\frac{1}{2}} \quad \text{(sample)}$$

In the example cited in **3** above:

$$s = (6.82)^{\frac{1}{2}}$$
$$= 2.61$$

5. The normal distribution.

The normal distribution is a mathematical function, the values of which are distributed symmetrically about their mean. The distribution is characteristic of many types of population, especially physical or biological ones. If the object of a research study possesses values which are "normally" distributed, its standard deviation will show the portion of values within a given range. For example, 68.27 per cent of all values will be within plus or minus one standard deviation of the mean (*see* Fig. 2).

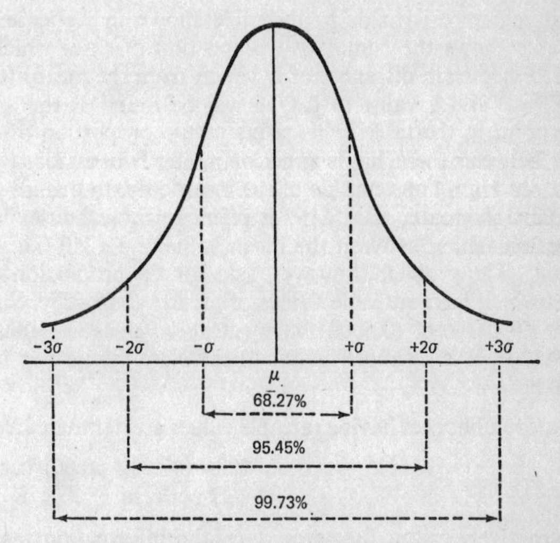

FIG. 2 *The normal distribution.*

The usefulness of the standard deviation can be illustrated in the following problem. Suppose that an analyst wants to know the percentage of individuals in a population who own houses which have rateable values of over £250. Analysis of rateable value records shows that the mean rateable value of private houses is £167 and that the standard deviation is £41.50. Assuming that the population of rateable values is normally distributed, the answer to the problem is calculated as follows.

First the *Z*-statistic is calculated (*Z* is the standard unit of measurement for a normal distribution).

$$Z = \frac{X-\mu}{\sigma}$$

$$= \frac{250-167}{41.5} \quad \text{or } \underline{\underline{2}}$$

where X = the maximum rateable value in which no interest is being shown;

μ = the mean value for the population.

Next reference is made to the table shown in Appendix III. The table shows the cumulative proportion of cases which are included at certain distances of Z values from the mean. In this case $Z = 2$ and a value of 0.4773 will be found at the appropriate point in the table. This refers to the proportion of cases falling between these limits (plus or minus two standard deviations, *see* Fig. 2) on one side of the mean only. In this instance, since £250 is greater than £167 it refers to those houses in the population falling between the mean value and £250 (i.e. 47.73 per cent). The problem, however, asks for the proportion of all houses which have rateable values of greater than £250. Since a further 50 per cent (0.5000) have rateable values less than the mean value, it is a simple matter to calculate the answer to the problem.

Proportion of houses having rateable values greater than £250

$$= 100-(47.73+50.00) \text{ per cent}$$
$$= 2.27 \text{ per cent}$$

Alternatively, given the same data, the information required may be the range of values associated with the 50 per cent of houses that straddle the mean of £167 rateable value (i.e. 25 per cent on either side of the mean rateable value). Referring to the table in Appendix III, it can be seen that the figure of 25 per cent (0.2500) either side of the mean is equated with ± 0.68 (Z values of σs).

Range of values: $\mu \pm 0.68\sigma$

$$= £167 \pm 0.68 \times 41.5$$
$$= £138.78 \text{ to } 195.22$$

NOTE: The Z value enables any value to be expressed in terms of the standard unit of measurement for a normal distribution, provided that the mean value and the standard deviation are also known.

6. Confidence limits and intervals. The analyst needs to examine every element in the population in order to make statements about characteristics of the population with absolute certainty. However, provided that he is prepared to tolerate a measure of uncertainty, the analyst can make statements about a population with certain degrees of confidence. He might, for example, say that the mean rateable value for all houses is between £138.78 and £195.22 and that he is 68 per cent confident of this being the case. In practice, executives need to have predictions which have at least a 90 per cent chance of certainty attached to them.

In the example shown in **5** above, it was assumed that all members of the population of houses were included when the mean and standard deviation were calculated. Hence, it could be said with certainty that the true mean rateable value was £167.00 (i.e. 100 per cent certainty). Suppose, however, that the figures for the mean and standard deviation were based upon a sample of 1000 houses. In this case it is very unlikely that the true population mean will be exactly £167.00. Under these circumstances it has to be accepted that the estimate is subject to error and allowance has to be made for this error.

7. Statistical errors. Statistical errors arise in the collection of data. They are different from arithmetical errors or errors which arise through lack of care in handling data. There are two categories of statistical error:

(*a*) *Random errors.* Those which arise from chance and are subject to the laws of probability. Such errors are always present in sample data and if sample observations are made at random, then errors will be normally distributed and their range can be defined with a given level of confidence.

(*b*) *Statistical bias.* This arises in small samples or where sampling techniques are incorrect. It is possible that a group of respondents may not be included in the sample when the presence of these respondents is relevant to the problem. Alternatively, the nature of the questionnaire or the interviewer may be such that respondents are unconsciously encouraged to favour a particular answer. Bias is most often found in non-random samples, and, if it is not detected and measured it can distort the analysis.

8. Estimation of the statistical error. It is possible to calculate the range of random error provided that observations include every element in a population. In this way the accuracy of a hypothesis and the precision of an estimate can be established. An estimate of the standard error of a population mean is given by the standard error of the sample mean. These two standard errors are denoted as follows:

$\sigma\mu$ = the standard error of the population mean;
$s\bar{X}$ = the standard error of the sample mean.

The standard error of the sample mean is a measure of how much the sample means, $\bar{X}$s, vary from the true value of the population mean, μ, due to random error. The formula for the standard error of the sample mean is:

$$s\bar{X} = \frac{s}{\sqrt{n}} \times \sqrt{\left(\frac{N-n}{N-1}\right)}$$

where $s\bar{X}$ = the standard error of the sample mean;
s = the standard deviation of the sample;
n = the number of elements in the sample;
N = the population size.

NOTE: It is possible to ignore the finite multiplier $\sqrt{\left(\frac{N-n}{N-1}\right)}$ where n is less than or equal to 0.1 N.

To calculate the size of possible random error for a given level of confidence the following procedure is adopted.

(*a*) When the sample size (n) is greater than or equal to 30.

$$\text{Error} = Z\,cl\,s\,\bar{X}$$

where Error = the magnitude of the possible random error (on either side of the sample mean);

Z = the Z-statistic;
cl = the confidence level.

(*b*) When the sample size (n) is less than or equal to 30.

$$\text{Error} = t\,cl\,s\,\bar{X}$$

where t = the t-statistic.

In computing the standard error in the case where proportions are involved, the standard error of a sample proportion is substituted for the standard error of the sample mean.

EXAMPLE:

(*a*) Compute the standard error of the estimate of the sample mean from a sample which yields a mean of 6.83 and a standard deviation of 3.27. The sample comprises 93 observations from an infinite population.

$$s\bar{X} = \frac{s}{\sqrt{n}}$$

$$= \frac{3.27}{\sqrt{93}}$$

$$= 0.339$$

That is, if the means of all possible samples drawn from this population were calculated, it is estimated that they would have a standard deviation of 0.339.

(*b*) Compute the standard error of the estimate of the sample proportion, $s\,p$, based upon a sample proportion of 51.7 per cent. The sample comprises 390 observations from a population of 5000.

$$s\,p = \left(\frac{pq}{n}\right)^{\frac{1}{2}}$$

where p = population proportion;
$q = 1-p$;
n = sample size.

NOTE: The sample proportion is substituted for the population proportion in the case where sample size is greater than 50.

$$s\,p = \left(\frac{0.517 \times (1-0.517)}{390}\right)^{\frac{1}{2}}$$

$$= 0.0253$$

That is, if a series of samples were to be taken from this population the standard deviation of the proportion would amount to 2.53.

(*c*) Compute 95 per cent confidence limits for the estimate of

(*i*) the population mean in (*a*) above; and
(*ii*) the population proportion in (*b*) above.

(*i*) Apply the formula:

$$\text{Error} = Z\,cl\,s\,\bar{X}$$

Now $Z\ cl$ at 95 per cent is 1.96 (*see* Appendix III) and $s\ \bar{X}$ is 0.339, from problem (*a*).
So,

$$\text{Error} = 1.96 \times 0.339$$
$$= 0.664$$

Now since the estimate of the mean, μ, is

$$= \bar{X} \pm \text{Error}$$

and $\bar{X}$ is 6.83 from problem (*a*), the 95 per cent confidence limits with respect to the estimate of the mean are:

$$6.83 \pm 0.66 \text{ to 2 decimal places}$$

That is, there is a 95 per cent chance that the true mean lies within the range 6.17 to 7.47.

(*ii*) Apply the formula:

$$\text{Error} = Z\ cl\ s\ p$$

Now $Z\ cl$ for 95 per cent is 1.96 and $s\ p = 0.0253$ from problem (*b*)
So,

$$\text{Error} = 1.96 \times 0.0253$$
$$= 0.0488$$

Now since the estimate of the population proportion, p, is

$$= p \pm \text{Error}$$

and p is 0.517 from problem (*b*) the 95 per cent confidence limits with respect to the estimate of the proportion are:

$$0.517 \pm 0.050 \text{ to 3 decimal places}$$

That is, there is a 95 per cent chance that the true proportion lies within the range 0.467 to 0.567, or, 46.8 per cent to 56.6 per cent.

NOTE: Where small samples of less than 30 are involved the t-statistic is substituted for the Z-statistic. For an understanding of the t-statistic *see* **9.**

9. The t-distribution. Once a sample size falls below 30 or more observations or cases, it rarely can be approximated by a "normal distribution" and it is inappropriate to use the Z-statistic. The t-distribution is very similar to the normal distribution but is influenced by sample size (or more precisely degrees of freedom). The degrees of freedom are the number of observations, n, less the number of "constraints" or "assumptions". For example, if 12 observations are made and their mean, $\bar{X}$, is computed, one degree of freedom is lost which means that 11 degrees of freedom are left. The *t*-statistic can be used in place of the *Z*-statistic to calculate the range of possible error associated with the estimate of the mean.

EXAMPLE: In a sample of 15 observations the *t*-statistic at the 95 per cent confidence level would be 2.145 (*see* Appendix IV) with 14 degrees of freedom.

If the sample, here, had a mean of 80 and a standard error of 9, substituting the *t*-statistic for the *Z*-statistic would suggest a possible error of:

$$\pm 2.145 \times 9 = \pm 19.31$$

Hence the true mean would be estimated, with 90 per cent confidence to be:

$$80 \pm 19.31$$

or between 60.69 and 99.31.

10. *F*-ratio. The *F*-ratio, or variance ratio, is the ratio between the variances of two samples.

$$F = \frac{s_1^2}{s_1^2}$$

where F = *F*-ratio;
s_1^2 = the variance of the first sample;
s_2^2 = the variance of the second sample.

In applying the *F*-ratio the larger variance is divided by the smaller one. The *F*-ratio is used to determine whether two samples differ significantly in terms of their variances.

EXAMPLE: Sample A comprises of 21 observations and sample B of 17 observations and the variances of the two samples are 4.0 and 3.2 respectively.

$$F = \frac{4.0}{3.2}$$

$$= 1.25$$

In interpreting this ratio attention has to be given to the degrees of freedom. In this example there are:

20 degrees of freedom $(21-1)$ for s_1^2
and 16 degrees of freedom $(17-1)$ for s_2^2

Referring to the table in Appendix V it will be seen that two sets of degrees of freedom are shown in the table. First proceed along the top of the table until 20 degrees of freedom is reached (the greater variance). Next look down that column until 16 degrees of freedom is reached (starting from the side of the table). At that point read off the two figures in the table:

2.28 (light faced type)	5 per cent level
3.25 (bold faced type)	1 per cent level

The statistic can be interpreted as follows. The *F*-ratio obtained in the example is less than either of the two values shown in the table. It cannot therefore be concluded that the variances differ significantly at these levels of significance. Had the ratio exceeded one or both of the values then it might have been concluded that there was a significant difference between the variances at the level indicated. That is, the actual ratio would only have occurred by chance either one or five times in a hundred as the case may be.

Applications of the *F*-test are shown in XII.

PROGRESS TEST 3

1. 6, 4, 3, 7, 8, 2, 5, 4, 9, 2, 8, 3, 4, 5, 2, 1, 0, 0, 4, 3, 2, 1, 7, 6, 5, 3, 1, 4

For the above data calculate:

(*a*) the mean;
(*b*) the median;
(*c*) the mode;
(*d*) the range;
(*e*) the variance;
(*f*) the sample variance of the first eight numbers;
(*g*) the standard deviation;
(*h*) the standard deviation of the first eight numbers. **(3, 4)**

2. Using the first eight numbers only of the array of numbers in problem 2 above, estimate the mean of the population (i.e. that array of numbers) with a 95 per cent confidence interval. **(5,6, 7,8)**

3. Compute the variance of the first eight numbers of the array shown in question 1, and, the variance of the last eight numbers in the same array. Could you conclude that both samples were drawn from the same population? **(9)**

CHAPTER IV

Sampling

1. Introduction. From statistics founded on information obtained from small groups inferences can be drawn concerning large groups. The smaller groups are termed samples. In this chapter the different methods of sampling are described and considered in some detail.

2. Census. This is to be distinguished from a sample survey in that it includes every member in the population. The principal advantage that a census has over a sample survey is its ability to remove all uncertainty about the object of the study by providing a complete picture of all responses. On the other hand, a census is for many purposes an uneconomic method of obtaining data.

In marketing research a census is often a suitable type of survey to conduct in an industrial marketing study. A manufacturer of jute materials handling equipment might well take a census of jute manufacturers to determine reaction in the industry to a new product idea. There are in total under twenty such manufacturers and it is therefore feasible to approach all the manufacturers concerned.

In the majority of cases the population of respondents is extremely large so that it is not practical to conduct a census. For example, a manufacturer wishing to test the effectiveness of a national advertising campaign could not possibly interview all those people who are likely to view the advertising.

3. Types of sample. There are two kinds of sample:

(*a*) *Probability samples*—in which each individual has a known chance of becoming a part of the sample.

(*b*) *Non-probability samples*—whereby there is no way of estimating the probability that each element is included in the sample.

Non-probability samples have the advantage of being convenient and economical, whereas the drawing of probability samples is apt to be expensive and laborious.

There are several kinds of probability sample. Two are:

(*a*) *Simple random sample*—if the names of each and every British employer could be written on to separate pieces of paper which were then put into a big revolving drum, then the probability of any employer's name being drawn out of the drum at random would be equal.

(*b*) *Stratified random sample*—in which the population is categorised into groups that are distinctly different from each other on relevant variables. If propensity to purchase a specific brand was considered to be related to different demographic characteristics such as age, sex and income, the sample would reflect these factors in its construction.

Non-probability samples are termed "incidental" or "accidental" samples. A manufacturer wishing to obtain a preliminary idea of customer response to the flavour of a new product may enlist the help of the firm's employees, because they are convenient. Such samples exhibit bias.

4. Deciding on the appropriate kind of sample to use. Simple random sampling procedures are employed relatively infrequently in marketing research. There are few problems which do not involve stratification of some kind. In the situation where a manufacturer is investigating consumer attitudes towards a new brand of nail varnish, the procedure of establishing a suitable sample could be as follows.

(*a*) The influence, if any, of male attitudes on the purchasing pattern of a female orientated product would have to be determined. If male attitudes are shown to have an effect, then males would have to be included in the sample.

Other types of criteria could be:

(*b*) different age groups of both men and women;
(*c*) social status as reflected in occupation/income group;
(*d*) the effect of marital status on both males and females.

Before proceeding to construct the sample the number of people in each category would have to be known. The sample should be drawn so that it is made up of the same proportions of the different categories as in the population from which it is drawn (*see also* disproportionate stratified random sampling in

11). This is then a case where a stratified random would be applicable.

If there were a study of user attitudes to a particular brand of washing powder it could be shown to be necessary to undertake an initial survey to determine the percentages of the population of users that can be termed "heavy", "medium" and "light" users.

A special variant of stratified random sampling employs a technique called cluster sampling. In this instance the population is viewed as a collection of groups that are much the same. Whilst, in normal stratified random sampling, selections are made at random within each stratum, in cluster sampling it is the clusters themselves which are selected at random. In gathering data on consumer attitudes to brands of washing powder on a nationwide basis, it would be possible to stratify the townships of a country on the basis of size and then select towns within each stratum at random. In each of the selected towns districts could be chosen at random. Streets could be similarly selected within each town. Individuals might be identified at random for interview or by "quota" until sufficient proportions of "heavy, medium and light" users were identified within each cluster.

Incidental or accidental sampling is employed when:

(*a*) it is the only method that can be adopted, for example, there may be difficulty in finding respondents.

(*b*) A very inexpensive survey is called for and the survey is intended to indicate the line a more detailed and expensive survey should take.

5. Selection of a sample. There are three problems which frequently arise in the selection of a sample:

(*a*) Every element in the population can seldom be identified or counted.

(*b*) Every element in the population seldom has a known probability of selection.

(*c*) The rate of response of elements selected for the sample is seldom one hundred per cent.

These problems can be overcome or minimised in the following manner:

(*a*) careful listing of members of the market population;
(*b*) random selection procedures;
(*c*) follow-up inquiries designed to reach non-respondents.

6. Representativeness. A sample should be representative of the population only with respect to those characteristics that are relevant to the study.

EXAMPLE: If a chocolate manufacturer were conducting a "taste test", the panel of respondents would have to be representative only in so far as their reactions to taste were concerned. If the distribution of income, family status or shopping habits of those in the sample differed from that of the population, it would be of no consequence.

7. Obtaining population lists. The list should include the name, address and telephone number (where appropriate) of each

Problem	Population List
Testing consumer acceptance of a new brand of toothpaste	None
Assessing customer price consciousness with regard to new cars	By recognising car registration plates with the most recent "letter". Sample is then stratified on the basis of new car price
Forecasting sales for a product range of machine tools	By identifying possible *end uses* and employing the *Kompass Directory* to identify possible customers
Problems in making first home purchases	Register of marriages – geographic sample
Views and attitudes towards religion	None – but care should be taken that predominantly "single" religion areas are recognised
Attitudes towards local radio advertising	Street interviews – no list
The public image of a local supermarket	House to house survey – voting list in town hall – sampled by district

FIG. 3 *Population lists suitable for a sample of problems.*

element in the population, *see* X. It is pointless to specify an exhaustive set of population lists since each will vary according to the nature of the problem. Figure 3, however, gives examples of problems and suggests population lists relevant to each problem. It will be noted in some cases that a population list is not required.

Some commonly used lists include:

(*a*) the electoral roll;
(*b*) local authority rates assessment lists;
(*c*) trade associations;
(*d*) professional organisations; and
some agencies have developed lists of industrial users.

METHODS OF DRAWING THE ELEMENTS OF A SAMPLE

8. Simple random sampling.

(*a*) *Equal interval method.* This involves selecting every ith element on the list, starting with one element between 1 and i (using random numbers). The interval is determined by the formula:

$$i = \frac{N}{n}$$

where i = the interval length;
N = the number of elements in the list;
n = the sample size.

EXAMPLE: A college has 3847 students and it is proposed to interview 281 students. The interval then is $\frac{3847}{281}$ (3847 divided by 281) or every 13th student (or alternate between every 13th and 14th student to be more accurate).

(*b*) *Random number method.* Proceed as follows:

(*i*) number the elements on the list $i \ldots n$;

(*ii*) select elements by reading numbers off from a table of random numbers or by generating them on a calculator or computer.

There are several variations of the basic random number technique. One is a multiple stage system. Here the population list is divided into equal parts, several of which are selected by the random number method. These "parts" are then used as the source of sample elements, which in turn are selected by the random number method. The variation is often used in conjunction with a telephone directory. Page numbers are selected and an equal number of names is drawn from each page using the random number method to make up the sample.

9. Stratified random sampling. Restricted sampling methods such as this divide the population into groups called strata. The elements within a particular group are the same with respect to the relevant population parameters. There are two ways of doing this:

(*a*) *Proportional sampling*. In this method sample elements are allocated among the strata in proportion to the relative sizes of the strata. A stratum representing 30 per cent of the population would provide 30 per cent of the sample.

(*b*) *Disproportionate sampling or optimal sampling*. This has the advantage over proportional sampling, in that it facilitates the minimisation of random error. To accomplish this more elements are drawn from the stratum with the largest standard deviation.

10. Proportional random sampling. A study of leisure-time activities might divide a market population into three strata: households with incomes below £4000 per annum; households with incomes between £4000 and £5000 per annum; and households with incomes over £5000 per annum. Incomes are used as the parameter to assign elements to appropriate strata.

Next a predetermined number of elements is chosen from each stratum. The object of proportional stratified sampling is to ensure representativeness by ensuring proper representation of each segment of the population (in the proportion found in the population), and providing greater precision than might be achieved using other sampling methods with the same size sample.

In this example, if 40 per cent of the population had incomes of less than £4000 per annum, then 40 per cent of the sample would comprise households with incomes of less than £4000 per annum. The same principal would apply to the other two strata.

11. Example of disproportionate or optimal sampling. In disproportionate sampling more elements are drawn from the stratum with the largest standard deviation (to make it more representative of the population). The total sample is allocated among the strata according to the following formula (*see* Walter B. Wentz. *Marketing Research: Management and Methods.* Harper & Row Ltd. 1972. Chapter 9):

$$n_i = \frac{W_i \sigma_i}{\Sigma(W_i.\sigma_i)} \times n$$

where n_i = the number of sample elements from stratum i;
W_i = the proportion of the population represented by stratum i;
σ_i = the standard deviation within stratum i;
n = the total sample size.

It is possible to modify the equation to include a cost factor (*see* Robert Ferber and P. F. Verdoorn. *Research Methods in Economics and Business.* Macmillan 1962, p. 245) i.e.

$$n_i = \frac{\dfrac{W_i \sigma_i}{(C_i)^{\frac{1}{2}}}}{\Sigma(W_i \sigma_i/(C_i)^{\frac{1}{2}}} \times n$$

where C = the cost of gathering data on a single member of stratum i.

12. Worked examples of proportional and disproportionate allocation of sampling elements.

(*a*) *Proportional allocation of sampling elements.* A sample size of 600 is assumed i.e., $n = 600$

Stratum i	*Income strata* £1000 p.a.	*Proportion in the population* W_i%	*Proportional allocation* $n\,(W_i)$
1	less than 2	21	126
2	2 under 4	27	162
3	4 under 6	23	138
4	6 under 8	19	114
5	8 under 10	7	42
6	10 and over	3	18
		100%	600

(*b*) *Disproportionate allocation of sampling elements* (*without costs*).

Stratum	*Income strata*	*Standard deviation of stratum i*	*Bring down W_i from (a) above*		
i	£1000 p.a.	σ_i	$W_i\,\sigma_i$	$\frac{W_i\,\sigma_i}{\Sigma(W_i\,\sigma_i)}$	$\frac{W_i\,\sigma_i}{\Sigma(W_i\,\sigma_i)} \times n$
1	less than 2	£50	10.5	0.0398	24
2	2 under 4	100	27.0	0.1025	61
3	4 under 6	200	46.0	0.1746	105
4	6 under 8	400	76.0	0.2884	173
5	8 under 10	800	56.0	0.2125	128
6	10 and over	1600	48.0	0.1822	109
		3150	263.5	1.0000	600

(c) Disproportionate allocation of sampling elements (with costs).

Stratum	*Income strata*	*Cost of gathering data*	*Bring down $W_i\sigma_i$ from (b) above*	
i	£1000 p.a.	C_i £ per interview	$\frac{W_i\sigma_i}{\sqrt{C_i}}$	$\frac{\frac{W_i\sigma_i}{\sqrt{C_i}}}{\Sigma\left(\frac{W_i\sigma_i}{\sqrt{C_i}}\right)} \times n$
1	less than 2	1.00	10.50	30
2	2 under 4	1.00	27.00	78
3	4 under 6	1.50	37.56	109
4	6 under 8	1.75	57.45	166
5	8 under 10	1.90	40.63	119
6	10 and over	2.00	33.94	98
			207.08	600

13. The standard error of the estimate of a stratified sample. The standard error of a sample mean, $\bar{X}$, when the mean is estimated from a stratified sample, is computed by one of the following formulae, according to the method of sampling. (*See* Walter B. Wentz.)

(*a*) Proportional sampling.

$$s\bar{X} = \left(\Sigma W_i^2 \left(\frac{N_i - n_i}{Ni\ 1}\right) \frac{\sigma_i^2}{n_i}\right)^{\frac{1}{2}}$$

NOTE: The finite multiplier, $\left(\frac{N_i - n_i}{N_i\ 1}\right)$, may be omitted where $n \geq 0.1N$.

where $s\bar{X}$ = the standard error of the sample mean;
$W_i = N_i/N$;
N = the size of the population;
n_i = the size of sample drawn from stratum i;
σ_i^2 = the true variance of stratum i.

(*b*) *Disproportionate or optimal sampling.*

$$s\bar{X} = \left(\frac{(W_i\sigma_i)^2}{n_i} - \frac{W_i\sigma_i^2}{N}\right)^{\frac{1}{2}}$$

where σ_i = the true standard deviation of stratum i.

EXAMPLE: Using data for proportionate allocation.

Stratum	*Income strata*	*Proportion in the population*					
i	£1000	W_i	W_i^2	σ_i	σ_i^2	n_i	$W_i^2\ (\sigma_i^2/n_i)$
1	less than 2	21	0.0441	50	2500	126	0.875
2	2 under 4	27	0.0729	100	10 000	162	4.500
3	4 under 6	23	0.0529	200	40 000	138	15.333
4	6 under 8	19	0.0361	400	160 000	114	50.666
5	8 under 10	7	0.0049	800	640 000	42	74.666
6	10 and over	3	0.0009	1600	2 560 000	18	128.000
						Σ600	274.040

$$s\bar{X} = \left(\Sigma W_i^2 \frac{\sigma_i^2}{n_i}\right)^{\frac{1}{2}}$$

NOTE: The finite multiplier is omitted.

$$= (274.04)^{\frac{1}{2}}$$
$$= 16.55$$

14. Cross stratification. Sometimes two or more parameters may be used to stratify the population; this is termed "cross-stratification". This is accomplished by:

(*a*) deciding what variables should be used to define the strata;

(*b*) deciding the strata to be used;
(*c*) allocating the population elements among the strata.

Once the population has been stratified, the sample may be drawn proportionately from each stratum or, it may be drawn disproportionately to minimise the standard error of the estimate.

15. Quota sampling. This is the most widely used sampling method in practice and if carried out with care can produce good results. Strictly speaking, since it is a method of non-probability sampling, statistical estimations based on data collected via quota sampling do not have a sound theoretical validity. For most practical purposes, however, statistical estimations from quota samples may be quite valid. It should be noted though that the results obtained from such samples are likely to be less valid than those obtained from a probability sample.

The researcher tries to obtain a sample that is similar to the population on some prespecified "control" characteristics. This may involve, as for instance in a consumer survey, trying to include in the sample persons in specific age categories. Half the people may be aged over 45 years and half less than 45 years of age. In this case "age" becomes a control characteristic. The researcher has to be aware of how the population of interest is divided in terms of the control characteristic.

In order to obtain a representative sample of the population a number of control characteristics are usually specified. The researcher includes in the sample a specific number of elements (e.g. respondents) with prespecified characteristics.

EXAMPLE

Two control characteristics are employed:

(1) Age. Two categories—under 45 and 45 years and over.
(2) Sex. Two categories—male and female.

There are four sampling cells:

(1) Female aged under 45. (2) Female aged over 45.
(3) Male aged under 45. (4) Male aged over 45.

The researcher knows or estimates the proportion in the population of interest to be as follows: (1) 18%. (2) 15%. (3) 42%. (4) 25%. Assuming the research involves a survey and there are to be 640 interviews, the interviewer will seek out:

(1) 18% of 640 = 115 females aged under 45
(2) 15% of 640 = 96 females aged over 45

(3) 42% of 640 = 269 males aged under 45
(4) 25% of 640 = 160 males aged over 45

The actual selection of the sample elements (respondents) is left to the judgment of the interviewer. He or she conducts the research until such time as sufficient respondents in each sample cell have been interviewed. Once sufficient numbers within a particular cell have been obtained subsequent encounters (e.g. potential respondents) are discarded.

In practice researchers have to exercise "control" on a number of characteristics. The selection of too many characteristics can create too many sampling cells and make the research impracticable to conduct. Caution has therefore to be exercised to avoid such a position arising. The researcher should determine what are the *major* characteristics which may have a bearing on the research.

DETERMINING THE SIZE OF THE SAMPLE

16. The general case. The best sample size is that which minimises the standard error of the estimate, assuming that accuracy is the prime criterion in research. However, it will be recalled (see I) that the cost of information is a major determinant of the quality and quantity of research that can be conducted. Accuracy can usually be increased by enlarging the sample. There will come a point, however, when the marginal increase in accuracy obtained in this way is not worth the additional expense of acquiring that accuracy.

There have been a number of formulae proposed to help establish the optimum sample size. In addition there are a number of different approaches to sampling which facilitate the drawing of a satisfactory sample size. Two formulae and the approaches applicable are discussed below.

17. Theoretical optimisation of sample size.

(*a*) *Simple random sample.* The following formula permits the calculation of the optimum sample size.

$$n = \left(\frac{Z\hat{\sigma}}{E}\right)^2$$

where n = sample size;
Z = Z-statistic corresponding to the desired confidence level;

$\hat{\sigma}$ = the estimated value of the standard deviation of the population parameter (usually estimated from a pilot study/survey);
E = the maximum acceptable magnitude of error.

EXAMPLE: An initial sample of some 50 rateable values of houses indicates a mean rateable value of £165 per annum and a standard deviation of £138. Establish the best size of sample to take to be 95 per cent certain of being within £5 of the true mean.

$$n = \left(\frac{1.96\ (138)}{5}\right)^2$$
$$= 2927$$

The best size of sample would appear to be 2927.

(*b*) *Stratified random sampling.* The following equation permits the calculation of the best sample size for a disproportionate random sample (*see* Walter B. Wentz):

$$n = \frac{(\Sigma W_i \sigma_i)^2 \times (Z)^2}{\sigma^2}$$

where n = the total sample size;
Z = the Z-statistic for the desired confidence level;
σ^2 = the variance of the total sample (specified as required);
σ_i = the standard deviation of stratum i;
W_i = Ni/N;
N_i = the total number of elements in stratum i;
N = the total number of elements in the population.

18. Sequential sampling. The practical approach to achieving the best sample size is to adopt some form of sequential sampling. This involves drawing a series of samples until one or more predetermined criteria are achieved. Such criteria might be:

(*a*) a particular number of elements in a stratified sample;
(*b*) a minimum confidence interval;
(*c*) any other desired value that is an unspecified function of sample size at the start of the survey.

The objective of sequential sampling is to use the smallest possible sample and still meet the survey design criteria.

"Quota sampling" is a specific application of sequential sampling to stratified sampling. Sequential sampling is employed until each stratum has the correct number of sample elements. The number of responses required for each stratum is determined by the methods shown in **11** and **12** above. If a disproportionate (or optimal) sample is sought an estimate will have to be made of the variance, σ_i^2, of the population statistic X_i, within each stratum. When a stratum is completed any additional questionnaires falling into that class are discarded. The survey is continued until the last quota is filled.

PROGRESS TEST 4

1. Distinguish between a census and a sample. **(2)**

2. Under what circumstances would you take:

(*a*) a simple random sample;
(*b*) a stratified random sample;
(*c*) a cluster sample;
(*d*) an accidental or incidental sample. **(4)**

3. When might cluster sampling be used? **(4)**

4. What sort of problems arise in selecting a sample? How might one try to overcome these problems? **(5)**

5. Differentiate between a simple random sample and a stratified random sample. **(8, 9)**

6. Suggest a means of drawing a sample to study each of the following:

(*a*) attitudes towards sterilised milk;
(*b*) future demand for a laser-powered can-opener;
(*c*) customer reaction to television advertising of hosiery;
(*d*) transport requirements (passenger) in the whole of the south-east of England. **(4–9)**

7. What do you understand by disproportionate sampling? Suggest how you would allocate sampling elements amongst strata in the following example.

Sample size 750.

i	*Age*	*Proportion in the population* %	*Standard deviation of the strata*
1	17–21	7	0.4
2	21–25	13	0.4
3	25–34	26	0.9
4	35–50	24	1.5
5	50 plus	30	4.8

(11)

8. Explain quota sampling. **(15)**

CHAPTER V

Consumer Buyer Behaviour and Marketing Research

1. Introduction. This chapter outlines the objectives of consumer behaviour analysis together with its application and contributions to marketing decision making. Methods of conducting this analysis are discussed, namely objective and projective techniques. Developments in consumer behaviour models are examined and their usefulness indicated. Finally, consumer panels are considered.

CONSUMER BEHAVIOUR ANALYSIS

2. Objectives of behaviour analysis. The principle aim of consumer behaviour analysis is to explain why consumers act in particular ways under certain circumstances. It tries to determine the factors that influence consumer behaviour, especially the economic, social and psychological aspects which can indicate the most favoured marketing mix that management should select. Consumer behaviour analysis helps to determine the direction that consumer behaviour is likely to take and to give another approach to estimating the potential size of a market, the segments within an industry, the preferred trends in product development, attributes of the alternative communications methods, etc. This data should help management to select the marketing mix most likely to achieve the required goals. (The marketing mix is the optimum combination of the elements concerned with the product; for example, range, price, quality of the product, the channels of distribution used and advertising communication methods.) Consumer behaviour analysis views the consumer as another variable in the marketing sequence, a variable that cannot be readily controlled and that will interpret the product or service not only in terms of the physical characteristics, but in the context of its image according to the social and psychological make up of that individual consumer (or group of consumers).

Economic theory has sought to establish relationships between selling prices, sales achieved and consumers' income. Similarly, advertising expenditure is frequently compared with sales. On other occasions financial accounting principles may be applied to analyse profit and losses. Management ratios, net profit before tax, liquidity and solvency ratios can all be investigated. Under all these situations the importance of the consumers' motivations, perceptions, attitudes and beliefs are largely ignored. The consumer is assumed to be "rational", that is, to react in the direction that would be suggested by economic theory and financial principles.

However, it is often apparent that consumer behaviour does not fall neatly into these expected patterns. It is for these reasons that consumer behaviour analysis is conducted as yet another tool to assess the complexities of marketing operations.

The main determinants of consumer behaviour are not only economic factors—for example, net disposable income (how much the consumer has available to spend on a particular product or service), or product criteria (such as intrinsic quality, availability, product range, colour, etc.)—but sociological considerations—including group influence and social environment; the attitudes of peers, class, family—and psychological attributes —such as individuals' predispositions—which all play their part in deciding whether or not the product or service is purchased, used and repurchased.

3. Individual needs. These can be considered at two levels, primary and secondary.

(*a*) *Primary needs.* These basic needs are essentially biogenic and include food, drink, sleep, sex and some degree of comfort.

(*b*) *Secondary needs.* These by contrast are psychogenic in nature derived from social, cultural, emotional and intellectual influences which could include the need for self-respect, status, prestige, etc.

Primary needs may in some instances be modified or overrun by secondary needs, so that it becomes progressively more difficult to differentiate between them as consumers are integrated into more highly developed and complex societies. Nevertheless, these factors directly affect consumer behaviour and therefore must be assessed in the most appropriate manner as defined by the confines of the marketing research, that is, financial, labour and time criteria.

4. Application of consumer behaviour analysis. The food industry is an example where this type of analysis could help to indicate the direction that marketing decisions should take. A recent survey of British eating habits (Mesdag, 1978) shows that in the food market not only has real expenditure increased by about 2 per cent in 1977 compared with the previous year but consumer buying patterns have changed. Some of these changes are direct consequences of a fall in consumer personal disposable income in 1974–5 which encouraged consumers to look for alternatives to expensive food. Real value purchases of canned food dropped as did frozen foods. Flour was bought for home baking at the expense of pre-baked goods, syrup replaced honey and jam, pasta products and rice were consumed in place of potatoes. Other changes have occurred, due not only to these economic influences but rather related to changes in social attitudes. With the high prices of fresh vegetables during 1975 frozen foods gained recognition as a value-for-money alternative. Growth in the frozen food sector has continued, not only among standard frozen food lines such as peas but even more so in the sweet (cakes, pastry, fruit pies and ice cream dessert) and ready-to-serve sectors. The growth in real sales of these products shows that it is much more than primary needs that are being satisfied. The need to impress the family and members of the social group to which the consumer wished to belong to satisfy secondary needs tends to outweigh purely rational purchasing when simpler, less expensive food would suffice. This change in eating has occurred despite a period of declining net disposable income and is contrary to pure economic theory predictions. Consumer behaviour analysis could elaborate on the reasons for this phenomenon.

ANALYTICAL TECHNIQUES

5. Methods of consumer behaviour analysis.

(*a*) *Objective techniques.* These methods assume that the consumer is both able and willing to reveal his behavioural patterns and to give the reasons for his actions. The researcher simply asks direct questions and accepts the answers at face value. Such techniques are effective in collecting factual information such as demographic, social and economic data. They are less effective for matters concerning a respondent's self-image (a personal view of oneself related to individual and group interaction), his attitudes or beliefs.

A typical example of objective technique's usage is the collection of census data, more especially the census of population.

Generally, a questionnaire with either a structured or semi-structured format is prepared (*see* VII). If the research is investigating matters that do not involve the respondent's self-image and if it does not have a high emotional content then the various objective techniques commonly used in marketing research can be employed. Personal face to face interviews, or perhaps, telephone person to person interviews may be applicable. A postal questionnaire survey may be favoured where anonymity is required for more sensitive topics, such as earnings, sex or personal hygiene.

(*b*) *Projective techniques.* These methods are essential in situations where the consumer is either unable or unwilling to reveal his behaviour patterns and cannot explain adequately the reasons for his actions. The techniques used centre around questioning the respondent about attitudes and opinions in an unobtrusive manner by enquiring about his attitudes towards a third party or an inanimate object. The frequently quoted classic example is the Nescafé study conducted by Mason Haire in 1950. The research first used an attitude survey based on objective questions to determine why the sales of instant coffee were falling. The straightforward questions were essentially: "Do you use instant coffee? If 'no', what do you dislike about it?" The leading answer was, "I do not like the flavour", which the researchers felt did not fully explain the situation.

The second stage in the enquiry used projective techniques to assess housewives' attitudes towards instant coffee. Two shopping lists were prepared which were identical except that one included Nescafé instant coffee whereas the other listed Maxwell House ground coffee. Two similar groups of 50 housewives were selected. The first was given the list including Nescafé instant coffee and the second the alternative list with the ground coffee. Personal interviews were conducted in which each housewife was asked to describe the type of woman who would have prepared the shopping list she had been given. It transpired that the instant coffee buyer was perceived in an unfavourable light, as lazy, disorganised and thriftless and was considered to be a poor housewife. On the other hand, the purchaser of ground coffee was seen as careful, thrifty and a good planner. Obviously, the simple answer which referred to dislike of the flavour had considerable hidden meaning that could only be found by the indirect interviewing methods used in projective techniques.

It is worth noting that a further stage of this investigation defined even more the differences attributed to the hypothetical shopper in each case. Although the validity of the Nescafé study has been questioned in later research (Hill, 1968), the study does show that objective techniques of consumer behaviour analysis can benefit from the application of projective techniques. However, it must be stressed that these techniques require considerable care in their implementation and interpretation.

APPLICATION OF CONSUMER BEHAVIOUR MODELS

6. Consumer behaviour models. It is apparent that consumer social and psychological characteristics play an important role in consumer purchasing patterns. Various researchers from the early 1960s onwards have tried to analyse the forces that come to play in consumer behaviour, to try to appreciate the complexities that affect marketing decisions. Models of consumer behaviour have been developed in an endeavour to illustrate the types of relationships that can operate.

Chisnall (1975) defines a model as "representing a theoretical construction of phenomena which are thought to be interrelated and significant in influencing the outcome of a specific situational problem". This could be the buying process in the marketing context. A model is then a framework or guide to researchers in marketing problems.

Models can be classified as subjective verbal models, decision process (logical flow) models or theoretical models according to the level of development. Sometimes, the latter two classifications are combined into one model.

(*a*) *Verbal models.* These are fairly simple descriptions of a particular behaviour situation as viewed by the individual. The consumer is asked, using either objective or projective techniques, to describe the processes his behaviour pattern follows to accomplish the purchase of a product or service.

(*b*) *Decision process models.* These analyse consumer behaviour patterns in more detail than verbal models. They show the logical steps taken that are highlighted in verbal models or in descriptions of activities given by the consumer direct to the model maker. One of the many examples is that by Kotler (*see* Fig. 4).

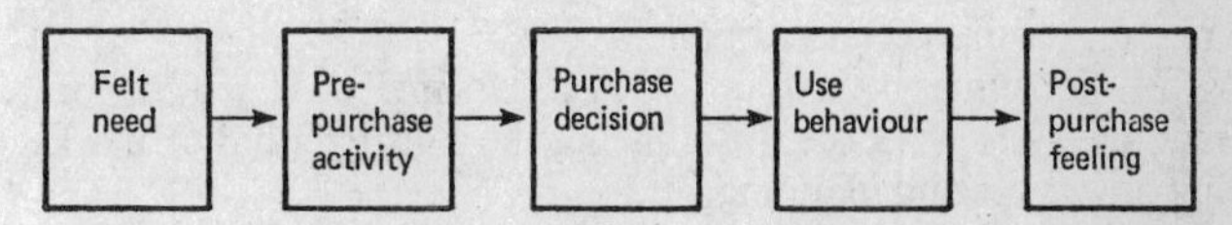

FIG. 4 *Kotler's decision process model.*

(*c*) *Theoretical models.* These have been developed from verbal and decision process models. They formalise the influences which affect purchase decisions and illustrate the extent of their interaction. Among the well-known models of consumer purchasing behaviour are those produced by Howard and Sheth (1969); Engel, Kollat and Blackwell (1968) and Nicosia (1968). These try to outline the affect sociological and psychological aspects have on the type of product that is placed on the market, for example, its shape and size, as well as its apparent image. Other models of consumer behaviour have been devised using mathematical and statistical terminology but as yet these are still very much at the theoretical stages of development. They have not so far been applied to real marketing problem solving situations.

7. Trends in consumer behaviour models. Marketing consumer behaviour models have certain general characteristics which were outlined by Sheth in 1976.

(*a*) They explicitly or implicitly believe in multiple controls and multiple effects.

(*b*) They are judged on the basis of external criteria, such as generating a targeted amount of profits or a rate of return on capital used. They are not assessed on their logical reasoning or their empirical validation which might be more applicable.

(*c*) The models represent aggregate relationships between control variables and market responses. They do not seek to understand individual differences, or, if they do, they presume the differences to have little significance.

(*d*) These models aim to establish the direction the consumer behaviour pursues as well as the magnitude of those relationships.

8. Advantages of consumer behaviour models.

(*a*) The models have emphasised that the consumers' psychological and sociological attributes act on the marketing product mix to provoke certain responses.

(*b*) Consumer behaviour theory has formally obliged corporate managers to appreciate the influence the consumer has on marketing objectives and planning.

9. Problems associated with consumer behaviour models.

(*a*) Both validity and reliability of models are, as yet, low. They cannot be used successfully for predictive purposes.

(*b*) There is still a lack of proper linkage between consumer behaviour theory and marketing mix policies.

(*c*) It is difficult to find top managers totally dedicated to customer orientated marketing. They are predominantly technically and financially orientated.

(*d*) There is a shortage of psychometric scales to measure accurately the aspects of psychological and sociological behaviour that are highlighted. The attitude scales that have been developed (*see* VI) are not very suitable.

(*e*) Expectations of model builders and users are too high. Models of consumer behaviour are intended as another tool for the marketing researcher rather than an answer in themselves.

Sheth further advocates that in the future, model building should shift its emphasis from producing optimisation models to building problem-input models (like that of his own). He feels that the display and communication of these models could be improved. Further, they should incorporate the ideas of market segmentation which are not encompassed at the moment. Thus, consumer behaviour models are useful marketing tools but require considerable development to be fully appreciated.

Details of the actual consumer behaviour models can be obtained from the references related to this chapter in the bibliography.

APPLICATION OF CONSUMER PANELS

10. Consumer panels. These are groups of people that are used to provide data on consumer behaviour, usually in consumer marketing research. The people comprising the panel are selected randomly as far as possible from the total population that is being investigated. The data obtained from this permanent sample can illustrate such behaviour patterns as the trends in purchasing behaviour. For example, the A. C. Nielson food panel supplies extensive data on product sales including types of food, brands, retail outlets and regional differences.

Media response can also be determined in this manner and can then influence any decisions of when and where to advertise. For example, under contract (at present until 1983) to the Joint Industry Committee for Television Audience/Advertising Research (JICTAR), the Marketing Research agency Audits of Great Britain (A.G.B.) determines audience levels. A.G.B. uses a combination of "diaries" kept by a sample of individual viewers of actual viewing times, and data recorded automatically by "setmeters" fitted to the TV sets in a sample of homes within each ITV region. These setmeters record "on" or "off" switching and channel changes only but not actual viewing times. Therefore, this is a measurement of TV usage only and does not account for the numbers of persons watching the programmes or advertisements, nor their subsequent buying behaviour.

11. Advantages of consumer panels.

(*a*) Changes in consumer behaviour can be assessed quickly under controlled conditions. The continuous record of behaviour provided by the panel enables the small trends in sales, viewing patterns, reading habits etc. to be noticed, whereas company records would take some time to assimilate these changes.

(*b*) Panel members are co-operative and will usually supply very complete data. However, as the remuneration, if any, is low compared to the effort involved, members of consumer panels do not remain on the panels for long periods of time. Two years is a common average period.

(*c*) Panels may be used under experimental conditions using different groups to compare reactions to treatments. For example, the effectiveness of a number of alternative new products or advertisement proposals can be tested under controlled conditions.

12. Disadvantages of consumer panels.

(*a*) The structured format of the questionnaire makes panels useless for exploratory research.

(*b*) The characteristics of the panel may change as members drop out from time to time, even though they are replaced by other members of the total population. There is a tendency to develop a "panel sophistication" situation, in which respondents become more aware of their behaviour patterns and overreact so that they are not typical of the total population.

(*c*) Members of the panel may adapt their behaviour to that which they feel is socially approved.

(*d*) Members, by virtue of their willingness to co-operate may have personality traits that make them atypical of the sample frame from which they have been selected.

13. Summary and conclusions. Consumer behaviour analysis endeavours to assess why potential purchasers react in the ways that they do with the intention of helping to predict consumer trends. Objective techniques are applicable where the data required is simple and in situations where it is unlikely that the respondent will subconsciously or otherwise distort the true situation because of social and psychological pressures. Objective techniques usually employ a structured, or semi-structured format questionnaire (*see* VI) which most frequently involves personal interviewing, sometimes the use of the telephone and, in studies about sensitive subjects, mail surveys. Consumer panels can be effectively used to assess trends in consumer behaviour patterns, especially for consumer mass markets.

In cases where the reasons for consumer behaviour are more complex projective techniques may be more appropriate. For example, if the subject matter being investigated is considered socially taboo or an indicator of social status where the family, social class and reference groups play a substantial part in consumer behaviour, direct questioning may not yield accurate results. Projective techniques ask the respondent indirectly to indicate his attitudes, beliefs, perceptions etc. towards a product, brand, advertisement or whatever. The techniques have been adapted from psychology and usually suggest that the respondent considers expected behaviour of a third party or inanimate object. The interpretation of this type of research is fraught with problems.

Consumer behaviour models have been developed to try to interpret this objective and projective data concisely; to illustrate the complexity of consumer behaviour and its direct effects on marketing decisions. Products or services may have certain specifications which in turn are interpreted by the consumer so that those products and services are given a particular image, for example, good quality, poor value for money, prestigious etc. However, it is the social and psychological aspects of the individual consumers or groups of consumers (or segments of the market) as well as constraints of time and finance that determine actual purchasing patterns.

Consumer panels can provide some indication of the actual purchasing patterns more efficiently and quickly than conventional company sales analysis.

PROGRESS TEST 5

1. What is the purpose of consumer behaviour analysis? **(2)**
2. What contribution can consumer behaviour analysis make to marketing decision-making? **(2, 4)**
3. How far can objective techniques of consumer behaviour analysis be applied in marketing research? **(5(*a*))**
4. When are projective techniques more suitable than objective techniques in consumer behaviour analysis? **(5(*b*))**
5. How useful are consumer behaviour models to marketing managers? **(6, 7, 8, 9)**
6. What are the major advantages and disadvantages of consumer behaviour models? **(8, 9)**
7. What kind of primary data can be obtained from the use of consumer panels? **(10, 11, 12)**
8. For what types of markets would consumer panels supply useful data? **(10, 11, 12)**

PART THREE
ACQUIRING DATA

CHAPTER VI
Measuring Buying Attitudes and Preferences

1. Introduction. This chapter discusses the nature of buyer attitudes and preferences and the methods of analysing those attitudes. The types of scales that can be used are considered, together with the problems of scaling and scoring that arise. Parametric and non-parametric data are defined. The chapter proceeds to describe the more common attitude scales that have been developed and indicates their suitability for use in marketing research.

2. Definition of an attitude. Gordon Allport (1935) defined an attitude as being "a mental and neural state of readiness, organised through experience, exerting a directive or dynamic influence upon the individual's response to all objects and situations with which it is related." It has been variously defined by other social psychologists but essentially it describes an individual's predisposition to interpret experiences subjectively according to his feelings which are themselves determined by social and pscyhological influences.

Attitudes are considered to be composed of components, and can therefore be measured in terms of different criteria. For example, a person's attitude towards child rearing may be the cumulation of opinions and views based on psychological and social influences (sometimes termed "constructs") which could include the individual's class, sex or nationality as well as economic factors such as family income, housing and educational background. Attitude scales have been developed to measure one particular dimension or aspect of an attitude (in which case the scale is unidimensional) or attitudes can be measured along a number of dimensions according to various criteria (in which case the scale is multidimensional).

3. Nature of buyer attitudes and preferences. When the marketing researcher starts to investigate consumer attitudes towards a product, a company, an advertising programme, a merchandising method, a channel of distribution or whatever, the initial data collected is often quantitative in nature. It could be an analysis of sales that highlights favoured product ranges, or the stage reached in the product's life cycle or even a company's market share position. However, as the marketing analysis proceeds the need to examine the qualitative aspects of buyer attitudes becomes more and more apparent, whether the company is operating in industrial or consumer markets. Sales analysis can show those products which are more profitable than others, but it cannot identify fully the reasons for this happening.

In the industrial markets it could be that attitudes related to safeguarding continual supplies have as much influence in the selection of which products to purchase as the specific attributes of the products themselves. The buyer may be prepared to use three or four manufacturers and pay higher costs per unit bought, rather than depend on a single supplier at a more favourable price. Alternatively, the industrial buyer may have a favourable attitude towards a particular brand of goods, not only because of the intrinsic qualities of the products but due also to effective public relations, or sales promotion on the part of the company concerned. Consumer loyalty so acquired will place the company's products in an advantageous position.

In the case of consumer goods customer attitudes influence the decision making processes as much as, if not more than, in the industrial market. Some of the many examples of buyer attitudes affecting marketing policies include:

(*a*) *A new product.* In early 1978 sales of skateboards soared rapidly among youngsters in Britain. The marketing research task is to assess not merely sales potential but to consider also the implications of the unfavourable attitudes towards the product of such groups as the medical profession, persons responsible for maintenance of law and order, or pedestrians. Adverse attitudes from these sources could affect future sales substantially unless they can be modified in some way.

(*b*) *A well-established product*. Consider a leading brand of breakfast cereal faced with strong competition from a new breakfast product, perhaps muesli, in the British market. The manufacturer of the traditional cereal has to study consumer attitudes and their eating habits related to breakfast cereals to be able to contemplate possible methods of coping with the competition.

4. Analysis of buyer attitudes and preferences. The investigation brief will establish the type of data to be collected. However, as more and more material is amassed it aids interpretation if it is classified in a manner that will enable comparisons to be made. It is for this purpose that attitude scales have been developed.

5. Types of scales. There are four types of scales used for the analysis of data:

(*a*) ratio scales;
(*b*) interval scales;
(*c*) ordinal scales;
(*d*) nominal scales.

The first two scales (ratio and interval) are particular cases using cardinal numbers and, as such, provide data which can be subjected to rigorous statistical analysis. Some data, especially qualitative data, can only be scaled in an ordinal or nominal form, but may then be analysed statistically (*see* III and XII). In addition, nominal and ordinal scales can be transformed into interval scales (*see below* **5**(*d*)).

(*a*) *Ratio scales.* These are series of gradations of equal intervals beginning at zero and each identified with a number. The numbers can be added, subtracted, multiplied or divided. The units of measurement are interchangeable. In this way, the same ratio scale may be used to measure different objects and the results will be directly comparable.

Common ratio scales include those for measuring length, volume, weight, speed and money. Thus, for example, feet and inches can be converted to metres and centimetres without altering the meaning of the scale. However, ratio scales can seldom measure behavioural traits.

(*b*) *Interval scales.* These are similar to ratio scales except that there is no zero. The zero point is set arbitrarily by the researcher. Intervals represent equal distances along the continuum being measured and units of measurement are again interchangeable. Like the ratio scales the numbers given to the various positions on the scale can be added or subtracted to obtain averages but they cannot be multiplied or divided in the same way as ratio scales.

(*c*) *Ordinal scales*. These are a ranking of alternatives. An ordinal scale is judged by the respondent who places each option or choice in an order of preference using ordinal values, that is, first, second, third and so on. These rankings indicate the order but not the degree of his assessments. The interval between the items is not measurable and is in no way equal as with the ratio and interval scales.

The ordinal scale compares the alternatives examined but does not establish the degree of preference either for the highest ranked choice or between the different items. For example, the respondent may consider a certain item more favourable but there is no way of measuring how much more so than the alternative. In fact, the most favoured item may not be sufficiently preferred to warrant the buyer choosing it in the real situation.

Ordinal scales may be of various types:

(*i*) *Differential scales*. The items considered form a gradation in which the individual agrees with only one or two items (or statements) relating to his position on the aspect of the attitude being gauged. He disagrees with statements on either side of those he has selected.

(*ii*) *Summated scales*. The individual indicates his agreement or disagreement with each item. His total score is computed by adding the subscores assigned to his responses to all separate statements.

(*iii*) *Cumulated series*. Theoretically, the individual will answer favourably all items up to a position on the attitude scale but will respond unfavourably to all subsequent items. In practice, it is particularly difficult to construct such a scale or series.

(*d*) *Nominal scales*. These are means of giving identities to words such as "yes" and "no", "very favourable", "unfavourable", "indifferent" so that the respondents' replies can be classified in numerical form. Frequently "1" and zero (and sometimes (+1) and (−1)) are the numbers used to represent the possible replies. The scores can be analysed statistically using chi-square and contingency tables. However, as the scores on nominal and ordinal scales have no "mean" value and no standard deviation they cannot be used in regression analysis as they have first to be transformed.

Some of the disadvantages of these scales may be overcome by transformation into an interval scale provided there is a reasonable number of potential respondents. The following example illustrates the method involved.

Three hundred men are questioned about their preference amongst five brands of beer. Each respondent is obliged to state which of two brands presented to him he prefers. All combinations of two brands from five are given to the respondent. The results might be as tabulated below, where the cell entries indicate the number of men who preferred the "column" to the "row" brand.

		Brand				
		A	B	C	D	E
	A	150	235	214	253	209
	B	65	150	146	148	139
Brand	C	86	154	150	174	180
	D	47	152	126	150	200
	E	91	161	120	100	150

n = 300

NOTE: The diagonal cells are given a value $\frac{n}{2}$. The matrix is then converted into a "proportion" matrix by dividing each cell by n (300).

that is:

		Brand				
		A	B	C	D	E
	A	0.50	0.78	0.71	0.84	0.70
	B	0.22	0.50	0.49	0.49	0.46
Brand	C	0.29	0.51	0.50	0.58	0.60
	D	0.16	0.51	0.42	0.50	0.67
	E	0.30	0.54	0.40	0.33	0.50

The "proportion" matrix is then converted into a "Z" matrix. This is accomplished by referring to the table of values of the normal distribution which relates proportion of area (p) to a standardised deviation from the mean of the distribution (Z). Thus, a p of 0.82 has an equivalent Z of 0.915; when $p = 0.5$ and $Z = 0$; for p values of less than 0.5 it is necessary to calculate $(1-p)$ and to treat this as a negative value of Z. For example, when $p = 0.17, q = 0.83$ and $Z = (-0.468)$.

		Brand				
		A	B	C	D	E
	A	0	0.772	0.550	0.995	0.525
	B	−0.772	0	−0.025	−0.025	−0.100
Brand	C	−0.550	−0.025	0	0.202	0.253
	D	−0.995	0.025	−0.202	0	0.440
	E	−0.525	0.100	−0.253	0.440	0
	Σ	−2.842	0.922	0.070	0.732	1.118
Mean	=	−0.568	0.184	0.014	0.146	0.244

The columns are summed and the mean for each column calculated. It is conventional to rescale the values obtained by giving the lowest value a score of 0 and correcting the other values accordingly. In this case by the addition of 0.568.

The new scale values for each brand are:

A = 0
B = 0.742
C = 0.572
D = 0.714
E = 0.812

If it is required, a nominal scale can be converted into an interval scale. This is accomplished in the following manner.

Suppose a nominal scale has two states which are "buy" and "not buy". These two states can be represented by an interval scaled variable which takes two values (1,0) where 1 = buy and 0 = not buy. If the number of states is increased to three which could be "buy often", "buy occasionally" and "not buy" these can be represented by creating a dummy variable. In this case two interval scaled variables each assuming the values (1,0) are used to represent the three states.

	VAR1	VAR2
Buy often	1	0
Buy occasionally	0	1
Do not buy	0	0

In a similar way it is possible to represent "*n*" states or nominal values with $(n-1)$ dummy variables.

Statistical analyses applicable to scale values are shown in the table below (Wentz, 1972 p. 279).

Type of scale	*Average scale value*	*Measurement of dispersion*	*Measurement of correlation*	*Test for statistical significance*
Nonparametric				
Nominal	Mode	None	Contingency	Chi-square test
Ordinal	Median	Percentiles	Rank-order	Sign test or Run test
Parametric Interval	Arithmetic mean	Standard deviation or average deviation	Ratio	*t*-test or *F*-test
Ratio	Geometric mean	Percentage deviation	All the above	All the above

6. Scaling problems. Choice of scale—the type of scale used is governed by the kind of information that is gathered and by the time and financial resources available. The scale selected has to be readily understood by the proposed respondents. It must be able to differentiate between respondents according to specified criteria, so that respondents with strongly favourable attitudes are identified as well as those unfavourably disposed towards the subject of the study. The strength of the attitude has to be ascertained if at all possible for, whilst it can be important to a manufacturer to know that there exists a favourable attitude towards purchasing a product, it is even more critical to determine the likelihood of the favourably inclined consumer purchasing the product.

Frequently the researcher starts by developing a trial or nominal scale. The scale is formulated so that the answer options are mutually exclusive. It has to be ensured that there are enough options to enable the respondents to express themselves adequately. It is possible that two options "yes" or "no", "good" or "bad" would suffice. On the other hand, many more choices such as "like", "dislike", "so-so", "very favourable", "unfavourable" may be more appropriate for studies requiring greater definition of the attitude. As the scale progresses from a simple two-option choice, it requires calibration to suit the type of scale developed and much behavioural analysis data will need to be rank ordered to facilitate the development of an ordinal scale. The equal intervals along both the ratio and interval scales will have to be defined, as will the zero point for a ratio scale.

7. Scoring problems. Buyer attitudes cannot be scored in the same way as in other behavioural tests such as those measuring I.Q., aptitude or achievement since there are no "right" or "wrong" answers. Further, the type of scale used imposes limits on how the attitude questionnaires can be scored. In the case of the most commonly employed type of attitude scale, the ordinal scale, the analyst can count the number of responses, but little else. Thus, in an investigation into attitudes towards alternative advertising proposals TV advertisement sequence A could achieve 60 per cent first place ratings, 30 per cent second place ratings, 10 per cent third place ratings and no fourth place ratings for content; while sequence B could attain 40 per cent first place ratings, 35 per cent second place and so on. But the attitude assessments for the same sequence might give sequence B preference over sequence A for another attribute of the attitude, perhaps, colour, novelty, attention or attraction.

Sometimes, the answers from several questionnaires, each measuring a different attribute of the attitude being examined, are scored for each question. These scores are then aggregated to give a numerical value to the respondent's test as a whole. In attitude scaling this method of scoring has to be contemplated with considerable caution. By implication it assumes that the scale intervals are equal (which is seldom the case with an ordinal scale) and, moreover, equal importance is given to each question. Alternatively, the questions can be weighted by numerical ratings to comply with the importance attached to their true ability to measure the attitude. This weighting is extremely difficult to accomplish without introducing bias.

The crux of the problem is to overcome the problems of changing qualitative responses such as "like/dislike", "favourable/most favourable" into quantitative ones. The coding process usually involves personal judgement which requires considerable skill if the parametric data necessary for quantitative analysis is to be attained. The meaningful analysis of non-parametric data presents numerous problems.

8. Parametric and non-parametric data.

(*a*) *Parametric data.* This is information measured in units that are interchangeable. Examples include length, weight, money and temperature. Ratio and interval scales are parametric. This type of quantitative data can be subjected to rigorous statistical analysis.

(*b*) *Non-parametric data.* By contrast, this type of data is measured in units which are not interchangeable such as value judgements, attitude and preference ratings. Nominal and ordinal scales are non-parametric.

ATTITUDE SCALES

9. Thurstone attitude scale (sometimes termed the "method of equal-appearing intervals" or the "Thurstone differential scale"). This scale, developed in 1929, is constructed to generate parametric data. Whilst it is doubtful that the scale provides genuine parametric data, at present this is the attitude scale most closely approximating an interval scale. The Thurstone scale is also unidimensional, measuring one particular attitude so that a new scale has to be constructed for each type of attitude it is to measure.

10. Steps for preparing a Thurstone scale. These are elaborate and time consuming as can be deduced from the following instructions:

(*a*) A large number of value-judgement statements (probably 50 to 300) relevant to the topic under investigation are assembled, preferably by a number of individuals.

(*b*) A panel of judges then groups the statements into an odd number of piles (usually eleven) arranged in series from "most favourable" to the "most unfavourable". The middle pile contains statements considered to be "neutral". Each judge sorts a complete set of statements. The piles represent the points on the scale and are presumed to be equal distances apart with respect to the degrees of favourability.

(*c*) The numbers 1, 2, 3 . . . *n* are given to the piles, starting with the most favourable. These numbers are scale values.

(*d*) The frequency distribution is noted and the mean or median is computed for each statement. Two statements are selected at random from each position (or pile) on the scale and the dispersion of their values is the basis for selection. A narrow dispersion (or spread) is favoured, as it indicates general consensus among the judges as to the statement's meaning and there is then a low probability that respondents will find it ambiguous.

11. Advantages and disadvantages of a Thurstone scale.

(*a*) *Advantages.*

(*i*) The scale has both nominal and interval values which are directly interchangeable.

(*ii*) The statements can be in the first or the third person making it applicable for either an objective or a projective attitude test (*see* V, **5**(*b*)).

(*b*) *Disadvantages.* The distribution of the statements along the scale depends on the judgement of the individual panel members. One way of minimising the effect of a prejudiced judge is to use a large panel of judges (perhaps more than 20) but this will increase the costs, in time and money, of formulating the scale.

12. Method of applying the Thurstone scale. The scale is generally administered by personal interview. The respondent is shown the statements in random order and without their numerical values. He is asked to assess all the statements and then to indicate those with which he agrees. The numerical values of his selections are averaged and their mean (or median if that was used in step (*d*)) value determines his position on the attitude scale.

The collection of scores represents the distribution of attitudes of the group of respondents which is usually a sample of the market population. The Thurstone scale attempts to be an interval scale, on which assumption the scores can be analysed mathematically and statistically. If the respondents are a representative sample, generalisations may be statistically extrapolated to the total population.

The quality of the raw data is suggested by the variance of the respondents' answers. If statements are selected by an individual that are widely distributed along the scale rather than clustered together it may indicate that for the respondent:

(*a*) the attitude is confused;
(*b*) the instructions were not fully appreciated;
(*c*) one or more of the statements were ambiguous;
(*d*) the scale was incorrectly calibrated.

If few respondents produce such score results their scores should be discarded, particularly when they have selected contradictory statements. If the problem is widespread, the scale itself will have to be re-assessed.

13. Likert attitude scale. The Likert scale (developed in 1932), like the Thurstone attitude scale, comprises a series of statements on which the respondent is asked to comment. However, the items or statements employed are in no way evenly distributed over the scale but instead only the extreme "definitely favourable" or "definitely unfavourable" scores are used. The neutral categories are ignored. Rather than examine in detail the statements with which the respondent agrees (and so further define the degree of favourableness of his attitude) the respondent proceeds through each statement indicating his agreement or disagreement. Likert used five categories to identify the respondent's level of agreement:

strongly agree; agree; uncertain; disagree; strongly disagree

On occasion more categories have been used (up to seven or eight) in later versions of the scale.

Each response is allocated a numerical score showing its favourableness or unfavourableness. The scores may be 1 to 5, with 1 at one extreme and 5 at the other, or alternatively the favourable responses are scored plus and the unfavourable responses, minus. So the following could be the scoring:

	strongly approve	*approve*	*uncertain*	*disapprove*	*strongly disapprove*
(*a*)	+2	+1	0	−1	−2
(*b*)	5	4	3	2	1

The algebraic summation in the case of (*a*) and the simple summation for (*b*) of the scores of each respondent's replies to all the separate items in the series gives his position on the attitude scale. For this reason, this type of scale is frequently termed a summated scale as opposed to the differential scale used for the Thurstone method.

14. Steps used in the Likert-type scale.

(*a*) The investigator assembles a large number of statements considered relevant to the attitude to be examined and which are distinctly favourable or unfavourable.

(*b*) These statements are given to a group of respondents representative of the population to be sampled by the questionnaire. The respondents indicate their answers to each statement by checking one of the categories of agreement or disagreement.

(*c*) The responses to the various statements are scored in a manner that will ensure the response indicating the most favourable attitude is given the highest score and vice versa. This may be done algebraically as with **13**(*a*) above, where the most favourable attitude would be scored (+2), or in **13**(*b*) where the scores would range from (+5) to (+1).

(*d*) Each respondent's total score is computed by adding his statement scores.

(*e*) The responses are analysed to determine which of the statements discriminate most clearly between the high scorers and the low scorers on the total scale. Statements that do not show a high correlation with the total score, or do not highlight differences between respondents with high or low scores (that is, extreme attitude differences) are eliminated. In this way the final attitude test may have quite a low number of statements.

15. Advantages and disadvantages of a Likert-type scale.

(*a*) *Advantages.*

(*i*) The Likert-type scale is considered to be simpler to construct than a Thurstone scale.

(*ii*) It enables the inclusion of statements that are not directly related to the attitude that is to be considered, contrary to the Thurstone scale. The statements have only to be found empirically consistent with the total score.

(*iii*) It is likely to be more reliable than a Thurstone scale of the same number of statements. The Likert scale enables a respondent to show his response along degrees of agreement–disagreement (usually five) whereas the Thurstone scale allows only a choice of two alternatives, agree–disagree.

(*iv*) The range of responses permitted to a statement in the Likert-type scale provides more precise data concerning the respondent's attitude.

(*b*) *Disadvantages.*

(*i*) The Likert scale is an ordinal scale only ranking individuals in terms of the favourableness of their attitudes towards a given object or idea. Despite initial appearances, the values are not equidistant along the attitude scale.

(*ii*) There is a tendency for respondents to opt for the middle value positions of the scale rather than to choose the extremes.

Values such as "uncertain", "agree", "disagree" are selected most frequently. Sometimes seven, or even eight, categories are used along the scale to try to reduce this effect. However, this may cause the respondent difficulties in mentally visualising and differentiating so many positions.

(*iii*) It is difficult to interpret the respondents' total scores. Respondents with different score patterns may achieve the same score and so be classified alongside one another, when in reality the attitudes expressed differ. This effect can occur with the Thurstone scale but is accentuated with a Likert-type scale where there are a greater number of response possibilities.

16. Q-sort technique. These techniques were developed in the late 1950s. The Q-sort attempts to group together respondents who have closely aligned attitudes. It is not an attitude scale but rather endeavours to differentiate between respondents along a simple agreement scale.

17. Method of devising a Q-sort.

(*a*) A large number (usually 50 to 100) of value-judgement statements relevant to the attitude that is to be examined are selected. The statements range from very favourable to very unfavourable and are normally distributed.

(*b*) An agreement scale with an odd number of positions is prepared. The middle point is the indifference (neutral) point. Each position is given a numerical value on a five point scale with values that could range from (+2) to (−2) with zero as the indifference point.

18. Method of applying the Q-sort. Administering a Q-sort survey can become involved and usually requires a personal interview which may be conducted with a group of respondents simultaneously.

(*a*) The respondent is asked to review all of the statements which may be printed on individual cards for convenience. The respondent has to distribute the statements among the positions on the agreement scale. He is usually required to assign a preset number of statements to each position to ensure a normal distribution of the statements along the scale, with the mid-point as the median.

(*b*) The answers are tallied by statement and respondent, frequently in matrix form.

(*c*) The respondents are clustered according to the similarity of their answer patterns. In this way those with similar attitude patterns are identified. Sometimes it is possible to categorise further the respondents into groups such as:

(*i*) those who are favourably disposed towards the subject;

(*ii*) those who are neutral;

(*iii*) those who are unfavourably disposed towards the subject.

(*d*) The appropriate analytical tests, such as analysis of variance, are made to identify any significant difference between categories and to ensure there is no significant difference within the categories.

19. Applications of Q-sorting. This method of measuring attitudes, by clustering together those individuals with similar attitudes and the identification of the individuals who differ from the norm has not been generally applied to marketing situations. However, theoretically, it can be envisaged that if it were to show that one or two factors had an influence on an attitude (for example, social class, income, shopping habits, television viewing) and that attitude was a significant determinant of the purchasing behaviour, then the Q-sort could be helpful in identifying consumers likely to possess these attributes.

20. Guttman attitude scale (scale analysis or the scalogram method). This scale, developed in 1950, aims to identify two components of attitude. It tries to evaluate general attitudes towards a product or brand (termed the "content" component of an attitude) as well as those attitudes directed at specific properties of the brand such as price, appearance, performance, taste and reliability (called the "intensity" component).

The Guttman attitude scale, like the Thurstone, Likert-type scales and the Q-sort, comprises a series of statements with which the respondent shows his agreement or disagreement. Unlike the differential and the summated scales, the Guttman attitude scale is a cumulative one. Statements are selected to measure attitudes so that response to succeeding statements can be inferred from the response given to a prior statement.

The Guttman technique endeavours to measure more precisely than other techniques the neutral areas of the attitude scale.

21. Method of applying the Guttman scale. The Guttman scale is complex in both application and interpretation.

(*a*) Respondents are first asked to answer a list of attitude questions concerning the topic that is to be considered.

(*b*) After each question is answered the respondent is asked, "How strongly do you feel about this?" to establish the intensity or level of feeling of the reply. Answers are classified as:

strongly agree; agree; undecided; disagree; strongly disagree

This determines the intensity component.

(*c*) The content component is computed by the intensity score multiplied by the score for the statements. In other words, the higher the number of favourable statements the higher the subject's score and vice versa.

(*d*) A "scalogram" board, which is a device to simplify the process of over-all analysis, is employed to analyse the scores of each respondent.

(*e*) The intensity scores are plotted against the content scores. These produce curves which are termed intensity curves. The shape of the curves indicates the distribution of the attitudes in a given population. A flat bottom "U" shaped curve shows a high proportion of neutral attitudes, while a sharply angled "V" shape highlights attitudes held by two strongly contrasting groups of respondents.

22. Advantages and disadvantages of the Guttman scale.

(*a*) *Advantages.* Although the preparation of the questionnaire together with the random selection of a sample of the population can be expensive in terms of labour and finance, the actual interviewing does not demand a high level of skill.

(*b*) *Disadvantages.*

(*i*) The method of selecting the initial set of attitude statements has been severely criticised. Guttman advised that the choice of suitable statements was made by intuition and experience. However, subsequent users of the scale have devised techniques of selecting a suitable set of statements which combines aspects of the Thurstone and the Likert-type techniques (White and Saltz, 1957).

(*ii*) The Guttman scale may not be the most effective way of measuring attitudes toward complex objects or for making predictions about behaviour in relation to such objects. A given scale may be suitable for one group of respondents but not for another group.

(*iii*) In practice this scale is seldom used in marketing research. In fact, the only well-reported application is an attitude study for the Shaeffer Pen Company conducted by Elizabeth Richards which was published in 1957.

23. Multidimensional scaling. This is a set of techniques that has been developed recently and which could, theoretically, be applied to the measurement of attitudes along more than one continuum. Numerous aspects of attitudes can be considered which are termed "space". It is conceivable that in marketing research these techniques could be used to investigate attitudes towards advertisements, products, tastes, brands etc.

Multidimensional scaling aims to take a single piece of data and from that to generate multiple measurements. The single piece of data is the ranking or matching of objects under investigation based on the personal judgements of respondents. The similarity between the objects is used to compute a mathematical model that defines the objects in multidimensional space.

24. Advantages and disadvantages of multidimensional scaling.

(*a*) *Advantages.*

(*i*) Psychological attributes of the object that is to be studied can be determined in considerable detail.

(*ii*) Market segments could be indicated and new product opportunities highlighted. It can be envisaged that with sufficient data, cluster analysis could be applied which would give more detailed analysis.

(*b*) *Disadvantages.*

(*i*) Multidimensional scaling has not yet been applied to marketing research problems. Numerous possible applications have been suggested which include evaluating advertising methods, the analysis of product life cycles and the segmentation of markets. However, problems associated with the development of sophisticated techniques and computer analysis coupled with the high costs entailed have curtailed its use to theoretical applications.

(*ii*) Problems can be foreseen in the definition of criteria for the labelling of the various aspects of attitudes that would be measured. The respondent chooses his own criteria for analysing his attitudes which could present difficulties in interpretation.

SUMMARY

25. Summary. One of the major determinants of consumer behaviour is the consumer's predisposition towards the product or service that is marketed. It is this attitude and preference that the marketing researcher endeavours to assess. Conventional questionnaires are unlikely to provide sufficient detail to understand an attitude fully and in consequence numerous attitude scales and techniques have been devised. The most frequently applied technique is the Likert-type scale, a derivation of a more complex attitude scale, the Thurstone scale. More recent developments have been the Q-sort technique which endeavours to group together respondents with closely similar attitudes, and the extremely involved Guttman and multidimensional scaling methods. The latter two systems have interesting theoretical possibilities but have had little use in marketing research.

The field of consumer behaviour attitude measurement has been investigated in countless ways with varying levels of success. However, as yet there is no fully satisfactory technique that is suitable for all marketing research attitude assessment. A technique has therefore still to be evolved that is fairly simple to apply and to administer, is relatively inexpensive and, ideally, has high reliability and validity in its measurement of consumer attitudes.

PROGRESS TEST 6

1. In which ways could an insurance company use a study of consumer attitudes towards its services to provide data that could aid marketing decision making? **(3)**

2. What are the four major categories of scales used for data analysis? How do they differ? Which are most appropriate for the analysis of consumer attitudes and preferences? **(5, 6)**

3. What problems can be encountered in the scaling and scoring of attitude scales? **(6, 7)**

4. How do parametric and non-parametric data differ? How can both types of data be applied in marketing research? **(8)**

5. How far does the Likert-type scale go towards overcoming the major criticisms applied to attitude scales? **(13)**

6. Is the study of buyer attitudes and preferences worthwhile? Are the tools (the attitude scales) that have been developed sufficiently effective to assess consumer attitudes? **(11, 15, 19, 22, 24)**

CHAPTER VII

Data Acquisition—Primary Data—Questionnaire Construction

1. Introduction. This chapter examines the use of questionnaires as a survey tool. The nature of questionnaire design and the importance of establishing a study brief to guide the investigation introduce the chapter. The major types of questionnaires are defined with illustrations of the design structures used in particular circumstances. Question content, phrasing, format, sequence and the physical characteristics of the questionnaire are discussed with special emphasis on the critical pretest stage.

QUESTIONNAIRE DESIGN

2. Nature of questionnaire design. Before considering the actual construction of the questionnaire, a brief should be drawn up and agreed by all the parties involved with the problem under investigation including the actual instigators of the study. A typical marketing research survey may involve representatives of the new product development department of a company, the company's marketing research department or an outside marketing research agency.

(*a*) *Brief.* The brief summarises the boundaries and constraints of the proposed study. In this way, all the personnel concerned in the implementation of the work fully appreciate such factors as:

(*i*) the purpose of the study;
(*ii*) the sponsors of the research and their specific interests;
(*iii*) the areas to be investigated;
(*iv*) the intended completion date for the study;
(*v*) whether or not it is to be a quick "broad-brush" study or an in-depth examination;
(*vi*) the financial limitations imposed on the research;
(*vii*) to whom the completion of the exercise is to be entrusted, that is, by "in-house" marketing research department

personnel, outside consultants, a trade association, an institute of higher education, or a combination of researchers.

(*b*) *Project design.* With the brief formulated and mutually understood by all the parties participating, the design of the project to be undertaken can be contemplated. The techniques employed could range from a large postal survey to detailed in-depth interviews. Group discussions may also be appropriate. The number of potential respondents will vary from fewer than ten to many thousands, according to the market under investigation. Whatever the method selected, the questionnaire ensures that the potential respondents are all asked the same questions in a like manner and order, thereby removing a possible bias in the study.

3. Definition of a questionnaire. A questionnaire is a list of questions or statements which require the interviewee to make a reply. These replies may be recorded either by the respondent himself or by the interviewer.

Questionnaires are one of the more commonly used tools for survey work and may be designed to elicit two types of responses:

(*a*) *Open-ended responses.* Here the question is constructed so that the format of the reply is relatively uncontrolled. The respondent is able to express his answer in his own vocabulary in as great a depth as he wishes.

(*b*) *Closed responses.* In this case the answer is recorded within certain previously defined types of replies. The language used and the depth of the reply is limited.

OPEN-ENDED RESPONSE QUESTIONS

4. Advantages and disadvantages of open-ended response questions.

(*a*) *Advantages.*

(*i*) They permit a wide range of replies.

(*ii*) They enable questions to be answered in considerable depth.

(*b*) *Disadvantages.*

(*i*) Large quantities of data can be amassed which may present logistical problems in the analysis stage.

(*ii*) Experienced interviewers and analysts may be required who are expensive.

(*iii*) It is seldom appropriate to use a computer to aid analysis.

5. Applications of open-ended response questions. These may be successfully used for the study of a small number of people in considerable depth. For example, in the market for commercial vehicle axles the number of major potential customers is under thirty. Each customer has particular product requirements which enables little standardisation to take place. In this case, open-ended response questions encourage interviewees to describe their own specific needs and problems in more detail than would be possible with closed response questions.

CLOSED RESPONSE QUESTIONS

6. Advantages and disadvantages of closed response questions.

(*a*) *Advantages.*

(*i*) The relative ease of interpretation of the replies allows the use of fairly unskilled analysts and, on occasion, computer analysis may be applicable.

(*ii*) They allow a large population to be covered at a comparatively low cost per unit.

(*b*) *Disadvantage.* They allow little detail to be given in the replies.

7. Applications of closed response questions. These are used when a large population has to be studied. This method is suitable in the initial stages (or search phases) of a survey where general questions with simple "yes" or "no" replies can select respondents warranting more detailed investigation. These respondents could be interviewed at a subsequent stage when an open-ended response questionnaire might be used.

8. General applications of both types of questions. Frequently, the same questionnaire construction has both types of response questions. The list of questions may commence with direct closed response questions but conclude with one or two open-ended response questions which provide the respondent with an opportunity to explain more fully his previous answers.

9. Example of usage of both types of questions. The market research programme for the Ford Fiesta small car conducted in the period 1972–6 incorporated many types of interviewing and used both types of question construction. The research consisted of three main phases:

(*a*) *Strategy research.* This provided guidance on the optimum small car concept and contributed to decisions about the favoured size, shape, interior space and mechanical configuration of the vehicle. It also enabled judgements to be made on the over-all viability of the programme.

(*b*) *The refinement of the chosen strategy car.* Information was sought concerning exterior styling, interior passenger space and major elements of interior design.

(*c*) *Final "detailing" of the car.* This stage gathered opinions on instrumentation, interior, trim etc.

Both open-ended and closed response questionnaires were used throughout the study.

10. Question content. In accord with the survey brief, the introductory questions endeavour to define the respondent as far as is practical and relevant. Personal details are often outlined at this point and may include the respondent's name, sex, marital status, age group, profession, number of children and home address. In the case of a company, data may be sought concerning company name and address, major company products, private or public ownership, number of employees and, possibly, details of total turnover of the company. However, questions of this nature should be kept to a minimum. They need to be carefully constructed and tactfully presented to ensure the respondent's co-operation, or the likelihood of his completing the questionnaire may be prejudiced. The sensitive questions concerned could be those related to income, age group, company turnover etc. and it may be politic to place some of them at the end of the questionnaire. This minimises the possibility of antagonising the respondent and any refusal to reply to the sensitive questions would not bias or otherwise affect the answers to the principal questions in the questionnaire.

Most, if not all, of the remaining questions cover the main topics highlighted in the brief. Check questions are frequently employed. These can be reiterated in a different format, and questions of no direct importance may be introduced into the questionnaire to try to establish the degree of reliability and validity of the replies to the central survey questions. Check questions are helpful when awkward subject matters are being studied.

The individual may over- (or under-) state replies to questions related to socially taboo topics and data related to a company's profits and pricing policies has a high probability of being inaccurately projected. However, check questions should be used with care and sparingly to avoid increasing the length of the questionnaire substantially.

11. Precoding of questionnaires for computer analysis. If the survey is to be conducted among a large number of respondents, or if a lengthy questionnaire with standard, closed response replies is required, it may be worthwhile considering the use of a computer. A computer can perform arithmetical operations, make simple decisions based on a prepared set of instructions and it can memorise data. Thus, it could reduce the time taken to complete the analysis and the expenditure on analysts' salaries. It is often possible to conduct computer assisted analysis in considerably greater detail over a much shorter time period than would be possible if manpower alone were used. Other situations where the use of a computer could be beneficial are those involving complex or unmanageable arithmetic, or simple mathematical operations which have to be frequently repeated.

In a questionnaire survey it may be that the majority (if not all) of the questions could be pre-coded. The computer would then be used to help analyse the replies and standard computer programmes are available for many operations. The computer could also effectively select a representative sample of potential respondents from a sample frame which could be a mailing list, the electoral register or the membership of a trade association. Other operations the computer can perform well include tallying the results of a large consumer survey, making statistical computations from the data amassed and sorting responses in accordance with specified criteria. These may be the respondents' class, age, or income; or a firm's product range, size or advertising expenditure.

12. Question phrasing. Questions should be succinct and unambiguous. The language used has to be readily understood by the proposed target audience.

The number of questions in the questionnaire will vary according to the type of respondent and the nature of the replies anticipated. For a survey of users of an industrial product, the kind of questionnaire chosen for an in-depth interview could consist of ten or fewer open-ended response questions; whereas, for a consumer product mass market survey, possibly conducted on a street corner, a questionnaire containing some ten to twenty closed response questions would be more appropriate. Up to thirty simple quick-answer questions may be used for a postal questionnaire for a mass market product. It is unusual to have more than thirty questions in a questionnaire.

13. Response format. Open-ended response questions beg for replies in two ways. Either the interviewee's thoughts are led in the desired direction by means of sentence completion, or a more direct question is asked. In both cases no indication of the reply required is given. For example:

I intend to buy this brand of soap because ____________________

____

Why do you buy this brand of soap? ____________________

____

Closed response questions indicate the choice of response that is anticipated. Typically, this involves a "yes" or "no" answer, with the possible outlet, "other answer, specify" or "do not know". However, it may be advisable to use a near equivalent to "do not know", rather than this actual phrase, to reduce the number of "do not know" responses and thus simplify the interpretation stage. In some survey designs it is preferable for the respondent to be given a wider choice of reply in which case it is usual to supply the units for the answers. For example:

Tick the appropriate box
Value in £

	Less than 500	501–1000	1001–1500	1501–2000	*More than* 2001
What price would you be prepared to pay for a fork-lift truck?	☐	☐	☐	☐	☐

	Very good	*Good*	*Fair*	*Not very good*	*Poor*
How do you rate the taste of this potato crisp?	☐	☐	☐	☐	☐

It is stressed that the format of the questionnaire must be presented in an easily read manner. The layout of the questions and answers should be vertically below one another. The questions should be on one side of the page and the space for the answers on the other. For example:

Question No.	*Question*	*Reply YES/NO*
1	Does your company purchase any type of plastic hosing?	
1(a)	If "no", Would you be likely to purchase plastic hosing in the foreseeable future?	
2	Does your company use other types of hosing?	______
2(a)	If "yes", please specify (e.g. rubber, glass).	______

14. Question sequence. The introductory questions define the individual or company responding. It may be advisable to place some of these questions at the end of the questionnaire if they are at all liable to affect the replies to other questions listed (*see* **10** above). Subsequent questions try to describe the topic area relevant to the study as agreed in the brief. They should place the respondent at ease and encourage him to complete the full questionnaire as accurately as he can and, if necessary, return it to the initiator.

Initial questions aim to classify the respondent into categories. They should be easy to understand, otherwise the respondent may be tempted to ignore the remaining questions and immediately throw the questionnaire into the nearest waste-paper bin.

The first survey questions (as opposed to the initial questions

Question No.	*Question*	*Tick where appropriate* YES	NO
1	Do you ever wear a tie or a cravat? If "no", skip to question 10	☐	☐
,			
,			
,			
,			
,			
10	Would you be likely to wear these types of neckwear in the foreseeable future?	☐	☐

Thank you for your help in this study.

which define the respondent) should indicate whether or not the respondent is able to answer the main survey questions. If he is not the type of respondent required, he should be taken to the last question and his involvement in the survey ended, if, for example, a man is to be asked his opinions about neck-wear (ties and cravats) the questions could be as in the example at the foot of p. 80.

The main section of any questionnaire should lead the respondent logically through the study topics. For example, a builders' merchant may be asked:

Question No.	*Question*	*Tick where appropriate* YES	NO
4	Do you purchase domestic chain?	☐	☐
4(a)	If "no", skip to question 10 at foot of the page		
4(b)	If "yes", continue with question 5		
5	Are you satisfied with the present sources of chain? In terms of		
	delivery time	☐	☐
	price	☐	☐
	quantity discounts	☐	☐
	reliability of supplies	☐	☐
	quality of material	☐	☐
	If "no", please specify	________	
		________	
,			
,			
,			
,			
,			
10	Do you envisage your company purchasing domestic chain in the next three to five years?	☐	☐

Thank you for your cooperation in this survey.
Please return the questionnaire in the prepaid, addressed envelope provided.

FORMAT OF THE QUESTIONNAIRE

15. Physical characteristics of the questionnaire.

(*a*) *Title*. The survey, or study, should be introduced in a manner likely to encourage potential respondents to co-operate but care should be taken not to influence the actual answers. A title helps to add order to the presentation of the questionnaire and it is often advisable to outline a summary of the reasons or aims of the study and to stress the investigators' credentials. This can be effectively shown by indicating the authority behind the survey and for this reason the questionnaire is commonly printed, or photocopied, on headed notepaper of the organisation that is making the enquiry.

(*b*) *Contents*. Confidentiality of the results must be stressed and adhered to, in keeping with the Code of Conduct for the Marketing Research Society and the Industrial Marketing Research Association (1976). The question sequence should be as indicated in **14** above. If applicable, the address to which the questionnaire has to be returned should be positioned at the end of the questionnaire.

(*c*) *Conclusion*. The respondent should be thanked for his help in the study. If there are any rewards for his co-operation, perhaps a free sample of the product under investigation or a company report, this should be presented promptly to avoid any possible ill-feeling. Sometimes it is the practice of a firm or government department to inform the respondent of summarised details of the results of a study, or at least, of where they will be published. It is then more likely that the respondents will help with further stages in the investigation or participate in other surveys conducted by other researchers.

16. Post Office services. The Post Office offers several special services for large users of the post which include the business reply service and freepost.

(*a*) *Business reply service*. For an annual fee of £15 a licence number is given which is printed on a business reply envelope (or post card) along with the sender's address. When the envelopes (or cards) are delivered to the addressee the postage (first or second class) plus ½p per item is due to the Post Office. The benefit to the user of the service is the considerable savings in postage since only the items returned are charged for postage and no postage due charges are incurred. There is also a saving in labour since stamps do not have to be physically stuck to each item and the survey takes on a far more professional appearance.

(*b*) *Freepost*. This is a similar service to the business reply service. The Post Office agrees to the use of an address which can be included in advertising and publicity material. Prospective customers can reply to it with their own stationery without using a stamp. The cost is ½p per item in addition to second class postage and the annual fee of £15 for the Freepost address.

PRETEST OPERATIONS

17. The pretest. This is the stage (or stages) in the questionnaire design when the questions selected are tested on a small number of the potential respondents or in a few cases, persons similar to the respondents to be used in the actual study. This stage indicates the questions with dubious significance, those which are ambiguous, and those which may create the wrong atmosphere in the questionnaire. The questionnaire itself needs to be tested (sometimes, with two, three or four separate versions) to ensure that the respondents are able to understand the questions and will answer them in the way envisaged by the investigators.

The pretest stages provide an opportunity for the sample frame to be substantiated using respondents of the type defined in the brief. Moreover, as a practice run for the real survey, the pretest identifies problem areas not previously considered. These can be associated with question construction as well as with the technical implementation of the survey. Frequently, at this stage it is found that the mechanics of the project have not been fully examined, for example, the postal survey demands envelopes into which the questionnaire will fit with the minimum number of folds.

The importance of the pretest stage cannot be sufficiently stressed. It is at this point that many errors in design and questionnaire construction can be appreciated and inexpensively rectified. The survey researchers cannot proceed to the full-scale survey until completely satisfied that the questionnaire is in its most suitable format.

18. Summary. Questionnaires are basically lists of questions. They are used in many marketing research investigations to gather primary data, including postal surveys, and are an important aid to interviewing. The questions will require either closed or open-ended responses, both of which may be difficult to interpret. Closed response questions seldom provide the investigator with sufficient detail, whereas open-ended response questions produce data which varies considerably in format, quantity and quality.

The pretest stage provides a valuable opportunity to test questionnaire design, phrasing and question sequence.

PROGRESS TEST 7

1. How important is a study brief in determining the design of the questionnaire? **(2)**

2. What are the applications of questions which elicit:
(*a*) open-ended responses;
(*b*) closed responses. **(3, 4, 5, 6, 7)**

3. Can computers be useful in questionnaire surveys? **(11)**

4. Design a questionnaire suitable for assessing the market for home insulation products among householders. **(13, 14, 15)**

5. Which post office services can be especially helpful for a postal questionnaire survey? **(16)**

6. Comment on the importance of the pretest stage in the development of a questionnaire. **(17)**

CHAPTER VIII

Data Acquisition—Interviewing

1. Introduction. This chapter defines interviewing and its applications to marketing research. It discusses the three types of questions that are used in the interview—structured, unstructured and semi-structured. Methods of face to face, depth, group and telephone interviewing are examined in detail and general techniques considered include the introduction, termination and interpretation of interviews. The chapter proceeds to identify favoured interviewer personalities and finally the important roles of supervision and training are studied.

2. What is interviewing? It is the manner in which an investigator (or interviewer) attempts to obtain information direct from a respondent (or interviewee). Sometimes respondents are questioned in groups rather than individually. In all cases the respondent (or group of respondents) is asked to supply qualitative or quantitative data related to the subject of the enquiry.

3. Why is interviewing used? There are three major reasons:

(*a*) to gain data not available from desk research;
(*b*) to supplement information obtained by desk research;
(*c*) to check or substantiate an hypothesis indicated by desk research.

4. Selection of the structure of questions used for interviews. When the possible format of an interviewing programme is examined, the investigator has first to consider whether the interview should be conducted in a formal, structured style or whether it should be allowed to proceed in an unstructured manner. It may be that a compromise semi-structured interview is most appropriate.

5. Structured question interview. Here the interviewer is provided with a questionnaire showing the precise construction of the questions to be asked. The potential respondent may be supplied with a copy of these questions either prior to, or at the time of, the interview. No divergence from the questions is permitted, nor can the order in which they are presented be altered. The responses have to be recorded within the criteria given which could be replies to closed or open-ended questions, or a combination of both (*see* VII).

(*a*) *Advantages.* Structured question interviews have the benefit of providing as much control as possible over the interview, thereby curtailing the directions in which the interview can proceed. This eases the problems of recording the respondents' replies and it helps in the interpretation of the results. It reduces bias between interviews and interviewers (especially within a large survey) as all interviews are conducted within the same limits. Costs incurred in structured interviews tend to be less than those for unstructured interviews since the interviewer need not be as experienced and the duration of the interview is frequently shorter.

(*b*) *Disadvantages.* There is little flexibility within the confines of the designed interview. Often, if the respondent had been allowed to explain more fully his answer the interpretation might have been easier and more accurate.

6. Unstructured question interview. Commonly this is a general enquiry into a topic of interest to the investigator. The discussion is defined within the interviewer's brief which should indicate the framework of the interview, highlighting features to be examined. The unstructured question interview allows the interviewer to pursue the fields in which the respondent may have expertise, interest or experience.

(*a*) *Advantages.* This type of interview can show sectors within the broad subject area that would benefit from further, more detailed, study. It is frequently used as a preliminary investigation tool prior to a full-scale survey and can elucidate problem zones such as taboo topics, likely biases, ease of obtaining co-operative respondents. This information will be of considerable assistance in determining the structure of the final study.

(*b*) *Disadvantages.* An unstructured question interview is extremely difficult to control and requires experienced interviewers if it is to be conducted effectively. The direction the discourse takes can easily proceed at a tangent to that which was originally envisaged. Considerable skill may be needed to return the discussion to the specified field and the duration of the interview may vary substantially. The accurate reporting of the respondents' comments can be demanding.

7. Semi-structured question interview. In order to balance the advantages and disadvantages of structured and unstructured question interviews it can be that the modified, or semi-structured question interview is appropriate. In other words, there is some definition of the interview topics to be considered and of the construction of at least some of the questions employed. Nevertheless, this type of interview can be flexible enough to incorporate any variations that may seem appropriate to the interviewer during the interview proceedings. For example, if the interviewer felt that a particular reply was contrary to expectations (or conflicted with other respondents' replies) that reply could be investigated during the semi-structured interview in greater depth than the original questionnaire advocated.

METHODS OF INTERVIEWING

8. Types of interview. Once the kind of questions to be used in the interview is established (either structured, unstructured or semi-structured) there is a choice of the interview method available. These may be:

(*a*) face to face (person to person) interviews;
(*b*) depth interviews;
(*c*) group interviews;
(*d*) telephone interviews.

These will now be considered individually in **9–19** inclusive.

9. Face to face interviews. Traditionally, interviewing has employed "face to face" methods of questioning the potential respondent (the term "person to person" is also used).

A typical example in marketing research is the interviewer in a shopping centre who asks a passer-by to answer a list of questions about recent purchases of consumer perishables (foodstuffs). This type of interview is unlikely to take much more than ten minutes to complete. Another application may be an interview conducted by a marketing research analyst with a marketing manager, perhaps of a building firm to consider trends in the construction industry. This kind of interview might involve a full morning or afternoon, or even, on occasion, the complete day.

The questions used in these face to face interviews may be structured, unstructured or semi-structured with the consequent advantages and disadvantages as discussed in **5–7** inclusive.

10. Depth interview. This is a variation on the general face to face interview method used in motivation research. It has been adapted from clinical techniques employed in psycho-analysis. The depth interview (sometimes termed the focused interview) is conducted in a free style, using unstructured and semi-structured questions, so that the respondent is encouraged to discuss the subject rather than to answer specific structured questions. The interviewer has a list of topics to consider and will guide the conversation in a general manner to ensure that each is dealt with adequately. Depth interviewing involves considerable skill to complete the interview without biasing the direction of the discussion and such an interview may take three hours or more to complete and a series of these interviews with the same respondent may be necessary.

11. Techniques. Some standard techniques have been developed to investigate motivation. Each demands responses to one of the following:

(*a*) word associations;
(*b*) construction of stories;
(*c*) completion of sentences or stories;
(*d*) arrangement or choice of pictures or verbal alternatives;
(*e*) expression through drawing or play acting.

Some of the more commonly used techniques are adaptations of the third person test and the thematic apperception test (TAT). Details of these projective techniques can be obtained from more extensive study of motivational research literature as shown in the reading list.

12. Advantage of depth interviews. This type of interview provides vast detail concerning the respondents' emotional decision-making processes. For example, subjective attitudes towards shopping in traditional department stores as opposed to discount warehouses could be analysed by these methods.

13. Disadvantages of depth interviews.

(*a*) Interviews may be prohibitively expensive.

(*i*) Costs can be high since expensive, trained psychoanalysts must be employed to conduct the interview.

(*ii*) The interview may have to be completed over a period of weeks.

(*iii*) Costs of finding respondents prepared to co-operate in the interview can be considerable. It may be necessary to provide the potential respondent with some kind of financial inducement.

(*b*) The results are liable to bias on account of the small size of the sample of potential respondents and the tendency for interviewers to interpret subjectively in accordance with their own particular interests and training.

(*c*) There can be problems in the interpretation of the large quantity of qualitative data that is amassed.

14. Group interview. Often, at the exploratory stage of a marketing research study, group discussions are undertaken to ascertain attitudes and motivations towards the subject under investigation. Face to face interviews are held in groups of six to eight members. Individual members in these groups tend to express their innermost feelings more freely than during a formal one to one interview. Thus, investigations into attitudes towards desk-top and electronic pocket calculators have discovered that members of group discussions voiced feelings towards calculators that would have posed problems in one to one interviews. Accountants felt that the size of the calculator was related to their own status and prestige. The larger the desk-top calculator the higher it was assumed was their own standing, or image. Conversely, it was believed that an electronic pocket calculator would adversely affect their image in their own eyes as well as in those of others. Hence, their attitudes towards the electronic pocket calculators were unfavourable in contrast to their attitudes to the larger desktop machines. On the other hand, for more mobile occupations such as salesmen, personal convenience and usefulness prompted favourable attitudes towards the pocket calculator.

15. Advantages of group interviews. Information concerned with individuals' attitudes and opinions can be obtained more readily than by other interview techniques.

16. Disadvantages of group interviews.

(*a*) *High costs are often involved.* These can include:

(*i*) The expense of using an experienced interviewer and some form of recorder (either a shorthand expert or tape-recording equipment).

(*ii*) The costs of managing the large numbers of people that are to comprise the group or groups.

(*iii*) The inducements to respondents to attend the discussion group.

(*b*) *Problems associated with the preparation of the groups.* These can range from the selection of the initial sample of members, to minimise bias, to ensuring the selected respondents attend the interview at the correct time and place. Even the choice of venue for the interview can itself pose considerable problems.

(*c*) *Interpretation of the discussion.* It can be difficult and is related to the success of the interviewer in directing the discussion.

(*d*) *Confidential information.* If a new product is to be examined, there may be problems of maintaining secrecy in the research stages.

17. Telephone interviews. The telephone provides a useful tool for interviewing, which enables direct person to person contact (although not face to face). The telephone can also be used in conjunction with other interview methods. For example, from the unduplicated version of the Yellow pages telephone directory (published by Thomson Ltd. for the G.P.O.) a sampling frame can be established from which the potential interviewees are selected. Telephone interviews can identify those interviewees that the marketing researcher would wish to interview in greater depth by face to face methods and may be supplementary procedures in other techniques of data collection. Thus, in a postal questionnaire survey the respondents who have failed to reply are interviewed by telephone to establish the reasons for the non-response.

The major difficulties encountered with telephone interviewing are:

(*a*) making contact with the desired interviewee;

(*b*) the introduction and explanation of the purpose of the study;

(*c*) the necessity to detail the investigation procedures concisely.

These problems can be overcome by sending, through the post, an advance communication to the potential respondent. This could take the form of a letter indicating some of the reasons for the study and the methods of its implementation. Frequently, a list of the actual questions or topics to be covered during the telephone interview will be included to enable the respondent to consider his replies. In this way, the respondent can be identified prior to the actual interview. For example, if the study requires that the person in control of the purchase of electrical cable at a firm be personally interviewed, the advance communication could be addressed to the Chief Engineer (or the Buyer). Hopefully, it will be passed to the most appropriate person who, in turn, will make preparations prior to the actual interview. In this way, wasteful time on the telephone can be minimised. Nevertheless, in some cases, where the questions to be asked are straightforward and few in number, it may be quite acceptable to interview by telephone with few introductory procedures, since it involves the respondent for only five minutes or so.

In a typical study into suppliers of motor components, the interviewer may make 30 or 40 telephone calls to all buyers of firms which use the components. Once the respondent is identified, the interview could proceed as follows:

		YES	*NO*
1	Does your firm purchase lorry cabs? If "no", turn to question 10 If "yes",	☐	☐
2	How many do you purchase per annum? Specify type	______	
3	What suppliers do you use?	______	
4	Would you be prepared to consider another supplier?	☐	☐
,			
,			
,			
,			
,			
10	Would your firm be likely to purchase lorry cabs in the next five years? If "yes", when?	☐ ______	☐

Thank you for your help. I appreciate the time you have given to the study.

18. Advantages of telephone interviews.

(*a*) *The speed with which the interview can be completed.*

(*i*) The answering of the telephone takes priority over all other business activities.

(*ii*) The interviewer saves travelling time and wastes no time waiting for the actual interview to take place.

(*b*) *Ease of obtaining an interview.* The respondent is flattered that he personally has been selected although occasional statements to the contrary are made. However, even in such cases, it has been found that apparently hostile respondents can seldom refuse a telephone interview whereas they will not grant any other type of interview (nor would they complete a postal questionnaire). This hesitation to co-operate may arise from a reluctance to provide confidential data, pressure of work or disinterest in the topic that is to be examined.

(*c*) *Costs.* Telephone interviews are usually considerably cheaper than face to face interviews, assuming that calls are carefully monitored.

19. Disadvantages of telephone interviews.

(*a*) *Sample frame.* Only persons, or firms, included in the telephone directory can be considered for the sample frame.

(*b*) *Cost of telephone calls.* Time taken to locate the potential respondent, which may take two or three separate telephone calls, and time to pass from the switchboard exchange to the particular person sought can be substantial. The duration of the interview has to be closely monitored, especially for long-distance telephone calls and at high peak-rate times.

(*c*) *No non-verbal communication.* Face to face interviews can provide more feedback than the verbal response of telephone interviews. In face to face situations the experienced interviewer can judge attitudes and opinions from the respondent's gestures and mannerisms. However, it is difficult to make these subjective assessments during telephone interviewing except by interpreting pauses and hesitations in the discourse.

(*d*) *Liability to interruptions.* The respondent in a telephone interview is not necessarily giving his full attention to his replies. He may be inclined to make the easiest answers rather than the most accurate in order to complete the telephone call as quickly as possible. Other persons may be in, or may enter, his room or office which will interfere with the respondent's reply.

(*e*) *Interviewer's voice and mannerisms.* The telephone interview does not offer the interviewer much non-verbal communication to indicate how best to conduct the interview. Once a particular approach is made, the respondent will note it and react accordingly. Moreover, the telephone can even distort or misrepresent mannerisms.

Sometimes a woman's voice can be more advantageous than a man's in telephone interviewing. In a typical industrial survey the majority of respondents will be male and they will usually be more co-operative towards a female interviewer. However, communication problems can arise over diction and the high pitch of women's voices. The telephone interviewer, male or female, has to be attuned to respondents' local dialect which is heavily stressed by the telephone. Telephone interviewing of consumer product users (such as housewives) is not prevalent in Britain.

TECHNIQUES USED IN THE INTERVIEW

20. Introduction to the interview. On the assumption that the interviewer has identified the prospective interviewee (or respondent) the interviewer must introduce himself either in his own name and/or that of the organisation he represents. Supplying this information adds an aura of authority to the interview which will establish it as part of a bona fide study, especially if the name is familiar to the respondent. Often the name of the instigator of the enquiry is withheld to avoid biasing the respondent's answers, but in those cases the interviewing agency can be identified.

The confidential nature of the results has to be stressed and maintained.

Usually at this stage the subject matter of the interview is briefly outlined. The method of recording the interview will be stated, personal note taking, questionnaire completion, the use of a tape-recorder, video-cassette or a third-party note taker. Tape-recording of interviews is becoming more prevalent. The interviewer can place a tape-recorder quite openly on the desk at the beginning of the interview and say, "I am afraid I am unable to write your answers down at the speed of conversation. Would you mind if I used this tape-recorder? It will enable me to concentrate on the interview and your replies. Thank you." It is seldom that the use of the tape-recorder will then be refused and its presence is soon forgotten during the interview.

The approximate duration of the interview must be mentioned and should be adhered to in the actual situation, or the respondent may feel obliged to terminate the lengthy interview prematurely. For most interviews it is advisable to ensure, as far as is practically possible, that there will be no interruptions during the proceedings. Such disturbances can range from a television programme distracting the respondent's attention to an apparently urgent telephone message which calls the respondent away from the interview altogether. It will be appreciated that these interruptions can affect results considerably.

21. Termination of the interview. The closing of an interview can be involved and may take five or ten minutes to complete. However, it is worth remembering the so-called "closed book technique" which can be very informative.

(*a*) *Closed book technique.* After the formal interview the respondent will noticeably relax. When the interviewer closes his notebooks, or appears to end the interview, the respondent will almost always wish to discuss the subject of the interview at length. At this point the respondent may elaborate on his interview replies and he may even divulge apparently confidential information (such as sales trends or new product development plans which would not have been given in the direct question and response situation). Unfortunately, it is seldom possible to re-open note books so the interviewer has to concentrate on the comments, which should be written down in the interview report as soon as the interviewer is outside the confines of the interview room. The information gathered in this way may on occasion be more helpful than the results of the formal interview.

22. Control of the interview. Problems range from the interviewer's difficulties associated with the recording of replies to the collation and interpretation of the actual responses. The replies can be recorded in full on tape or with the help of shorthand. Alternatively, they may be summarised by the interviewer or categorised according to predetermined criteria defined in the questionnaire. Nevertheless, no matter how well constructed and tested the questionnaire, or how well briefed the interviewer, the replies obtained can indicate that the respondent has misinterpreted the question. It is recommended in such circumstances that the interviewer should repeat the question in the original format, perhaps giving an indication of the units in which the answer is anticipated. For example:

	Every day	*Once a week*	*Fortnightly*	*Less than every two weeks*
How frequently do you go shopping?	☐	☐	☐	☐

Only as a last resort would the interviewer reconstruct the question and then the actual question structure should be noted for the analysis stage. In extreme cases the interview procedures laid down in the brief may demand that another respondent is selected. It can help considerably in the analysis of the interview if the interviewer records extraneous (but relevant) comments made by the respondent during the interview, either at the end of the questionnaire or report or alongside the particular question if that is more applicable.

The interpretation of unstructured interviews is demanding and should be undertaken only by experienced researchers. It is advised that, where at all feasible, the interviewers should analyse the results. This may not be practical with a large number of interviewers or when interviewers with local knowledge, language or dialect are employed, and in such cases the replies should be recorded in full. It should be recognised that the time taken to analyse an interview recorded on tape can take no less than the duration of the recording.

INTERVIEWER CHARACTERISTICS

23. Selection of interviewers.

(*a*) *Personality*. It is not easy to interview effectively. Ideally, the interviewer should have certain personality attributes. He, or she, should be:

(*i*) *a good listener*. The interviewer must allow the respondent to express his or her own opinions and attitudes whether or not they correspond to those views held by the interviewer;

(*ii*) *able to record accurately the replies given*. The interviewer has to avoid the cognitive dissonance effect which could lead to a tendency to note feelings and expressions most closely aligned to his own, as opposed to those that contradict his beliefs;

(*iii*) *systematic and thorough.* The interviewer must not skip corners either when selecting the potential respondent or when undertaking the interview, or at any other stage of the investigation;

(*iv*) *likely to encourage the respondent to reply to the best of his ability.* Many respondents lack the confidence to answer the questions asked. For example, frequently a housewife suggests that her husband should take her place. Further, during the interview the respondent's interest may flag and, in that case, the interviewer should tactfully encourage, possibly by speaking more quickly, by varying the tone of voice used or maybe by saying, "Only a few more questions to go" (if that is true) or "Over half-way now" (if that is the situation);

(*v*) *disciplined.* The interviewer must comply with the constraints given in the interview brief. If the selection procedures laid down determine that the respondent must have certain predetermined characteristics, then the interviewer must conduct the interview only with a person that falls within that category. Thus, if a housewife aged between 30 and 35 years, with two children is required, a near equivalent such as a housewife with one child would not suffice.

(*b*) *Sex.* Women conduct most of the interviewing in consumer marketing research in the U.K. Male interviewers are used the most in studies into industrial product markets but these involve fewer interviewers. The greater use of women may be attributed to various factors. Women are rather better listeners than men due to cultural and social pressures. Moreover, women, especially married women, are willing to work on a part-time basis (including evening work) and have until recently been prepared to accept lower rates of pay than their male counterparts. It remains to be seen whether the Sex Discrimination Act of 1975 will reverse these trends. A further advantage of women is that they are more willing than men to conduct the interview in strict accordance with the brief. Thus, over a period of time they are less tempted to alter the interview procedures or the questionnaire structure.

Nevertheless, traditions are changing. Men interviewers are being employed in consumer studies, especially for opinion poll enquiries, whilst in industrial fields women interviewers are more numerous than previously. In the industrial survey interview situation the interviewer, whether man or woman, may be expected to possess considerable technical knowledge, or at least, will have to be thoroughly briefed in the subject of the study to be able to interview effectively. It is this expertise that is more significant than the sex of the interviewer. In fact, assuming the interviewer is competent in the field of the enquiry, it has been found that women interviewers in industrial marketing studies can be more successful than men both in obtaining interviews and in the implementation of the interview (Aucamp, 1973). The majority of respondents encountered in industrial marketing research are male. They are extremely curious to meet a woman interviewer. Once in the interview situation, the respondent is inclined to be sympathetic to the lady interviewer which leads to good co-operation on his behalf.

(*c*) *Personal presentation.* The interviewer must have a neat, efficient disposition. Dress style should not detract from the interview discussions (Argyle, 1967).

To summarise, interviewers need to possess certain personality traits. They should be pleasant, have quiet mannerisms, good listening abilities and they must be reliable. Sometimes particular knowledge and expertise are desirable and, on occasion, being female can be advantageous. Even so, supervision and training are of paramount importance to ensure accurate and effective interviewing.

INTERVIEWER SUPERVISION AND TRAINING

24. Supervision of interviewers. The marketing research interviewer faces many of the problems experienced by salesmen. Interviewers are conducted individually (albeit the interviewer may be a member of an interviewing team in large scale exercises) and require that the interviewer should exhibit considerable self-motivation and self-sufficiency. Effective supervision is essential to ensure that the interviewer appreciates the full significance of the accurate selection of the sample of respondents, the importance of precise recording of the interview and the prompt dispatch of the completed questionnaires (or interview tapes etc.).

Good supervision provides the interviewer working in isolation with a feeling of belonging to a team. It helps to achieve high morale and enthusiasm for the project which in turn acts as a control over the interviewer's behaviour. Supervisors usually explain the purpose of the study although care has to be exercised not to bias the results by indicating what might be expected. Some research procedures incorporate incentives, often financial, to encourage the interviewer to complete the optimum number of interviews, but checks have to be made to prevent deterioration in the quality of the interview or even the fabrication of interviews. Random checks on actual interviews professed to have been completed may be appropriate, or the interviewer can be cross-examined for further explanation of the interview.

Not only does the supervisor control the interviewers, but he (or she) also acts on anomalies or comments highlighted by the interviewer. These observations can be very important and may even indicate that a programme of interviews should be curtailed, or stopped altogether, until further assessment is possible. For example, a question might be repeatedly misinterpreted or some questions could refer to conditions that no longer prevail in the market. The interviewer appreciates this situation from the replies recorded and should report them to the supervisor.

25. Training of interviewers. Training aims to illustrate to prospective interviewers exactly what activities have to be conducted. The interviewer is introduced to various types of interview situations; unstructured, structured, or semi-structured question interviews, depth, group and telephone interviews and the special techniques applicable. The trainee interviewer should observe interviews conducted by experienced interviewers. Mock-up trials may be used in the early stages but ultimately real cases must be employed. Useful practice can be achieved by serving an apprenticeship as a note-taker (or tape-recorder operator) at these interviews.

In addition to the actual interview techniques the stages leading up to and terminating an interview must be learnt. Further, personal presentation and mannerisms have to be cultivated.

Steps in the training programme will show the trainee:

(*a*) how the interviewee is selected;
(*b*) how the interview is obtained;
(*c*) how the interview is opened and closed;
(*d*) how to avoid antagonising the potential respondent;
(*e*) how to prevent bias in the interview situation;

(*f*) how to provide for the possibility of a subsequent interview with the same respondent.

26. Future trends. In the future it can be envisaged that the telex system could be appropriate for industrial product studies or international investigations providing access to the desired sample of respondents can be ensured. The use of a TV channel or a radio programme for marketing research studies have also been considered but seem impractical at present.

27. Summary. Interviewing is one of the most commonly used methods of obtaining primary data. Essentially, an interviewer discusses with a respondent predetermined topics which use structured, unstructured or semi-structured questions. The type of interview (face to face, depth, group or telephone) conducted is determined by the kind of information that is sought and the constraints placed on the investigation in terms of financial and time limits. In some situations one method of interviewing will suffice, whereas in others a combination, or all, of the methods may be necessary.

Good interviewing requires interviewers with certain personality characteristics which include reliability, discipline and the ability to listen. Most of these attributes can be learned with the application of effective supervision, training and control.

PROGRESS TEST 8

1. What type of question interview structure (or combination of questions) would you use for the following types of market investigations, structured, unstructured or semi-structured?

The assessment of the markets for:

(*a*) a new range of cars;

(*b*) fashion clothes;

(*c*) fitted kitchen units;

(*d*) bread or cakes;

(*e*) agricultural tractor accessories. **(5, 6, 7)**

2. Under what circumstances would group interviewing be applicable? **(14, 15, 16)**

3. How far can telephone interviewing help to reduce the costs of traditional face to face interviewing? **(17, 18, 19)**

4. Discuss the relative advantages of male or female interviewers under the following situations:

(*a*) housewives for a survey of food purchases;
(*b*) car drivers during a traffic census;
(*c*) tourist at a border control on travel habits;
(*d*) building contractors on the use of a new building material.
(23)

5. To what extent can supervision and training control possible interview bias? **(24, 25)**

CHAPTER IX

Acquisition of Data—Experimentation

1. Introduction. In this chapter the various types of experimental research designs which can be applied to marketing experiments are examined. Experimentation involves the deliberate manipulation of one or more variables by the experimenter in such a way that its effect upon one or more other variables can be measured. Some examples of marketing experiments are:

(*a*) measuring the effectiveness of different points of purchase promotional material;

(*b*) assessing the impact on sales of additional salesmen's bonuses for certain products;

(*c*) estimating the impact on sales of a product by varying its price to the customer.

Experiments attempt to establish and measure causal relationships among variables under consideration. Moreover, they must be carefully designed to avoid a number of types of experimental error.

2. Experimentation objectives. It is often difficult to assess the relationship between marketing strategy and/or tactics with sales or some other factor as it arises in the actual situation. For example, it may be a complex decision to determine whether it is more effective to display goods of a particular kind in one part of a store rather than another. Furthermore, it is hard to assess the effectiveness of some marketing aids; for example, the "eye-catching" appeal of a display unit. So many circumstances may influence consumer reactions and purchasing rates that establishing precisely the variables and then relationships can be extremely demanding.

The object of an experiment is to overcome the problems of measuring cause and effect by controlling for those factors which in real life distort a relationship. Sometimes, of course, experimentation is a mean of testing reality in advance—for example, in the launching of a new product.

3. Limitations of marketing experimentation. A marketing experiment does not necessarily mean that something is performed away from the real life situation, although it does sometimes happen. The measurement of advertising recall may take place at a gathering of specially invited participants. Package preferences or "taste" preferences may be measured in an artificial situation similar to the actual one. In those circumstances, consumers are being observed or tested under environmental conditions which do not reflect the real life situation. In consequence, it may be that experimental results are atypical of what would happen in reality.

In some instances the experiment is conducted in the real life situation. Experimental treatment of shelf space and height above the floor of the store are good examples. In such cases the objective is to relate both these variables to sales of a product. These situations remove the artificiality of the experimental environment problem mentioned above.

Experiments often involve relatively small samples of the total population. It is possible therefore that generalisation to the total market of the experimental findings may not always be fruitful.

SOURCES OF ERROR AND BASIC DESIGN

4. Types of experimental errors. In order that an experiment is useful, care must be taken to ensure that all sources of error are eliminated. Such possible sources of error are as follows:

(*a*) *Premeasurement.* Experiments may involve approaching people and posing questions to them prior to obtaining their co-operation in an experiment. This may have the effect of making the subjects over-sensitive to the experiment. Premeasurement effects can happen any time the taking of a prior-measurement (or even talking to respondents about the purpose of the study) has a direct effect on the performance in a subsequent measurement.

(*b*) *Maturation.* Respondents may alter their responses to a specific stimulant over a period of time, irrespective of external events. In a prolonged "taste testing" experiment, respondents may become thirstier as the experiment progresses and this may affect their response to a particular flavour. Maturation is a considerable problem in instances where experiments are protracted.

(*c*) *Time lapse.* Here experimental errors may occur when any variables or events, other than the ones manipulated by the experimenter, take place between the pre- and post-measures, thereby affecting the value of the dependent variable. For example, suppose an experiment is arranged in a supermarket to test the sales creating effectiveness of a particular premium offer on product X. After the experiment has begun a special in-store promotional campaign might be mounted by a rival company. The true sales creating potential of the premium would be likely to be distorted by the extra promotion of the rival brand.

(*d*) *Instrumentation.* Error can arise because the measuring instruments themselves may change with the passage of time. The interest and involvement of the people engaged in the research may wane as time passes, which may effect the manner in which the research is conducted.

(*e*) *Selection.* Errors can be encountered when the groups formed for the purpose of an experiment are initially unequal with respect to the dependent variable or with respect to their propensity to respond to the independent variable. The pretesting of an advertising campaign with predominantly male appeal may be distorted if respondents are predominantly male or female.

(*f*) *Mortality.* After a period of time, respondents in an experiment may refuse to continue their participation. The experimental results at a later stage in the experiment may not be representative of what might have emerged had all the original respondents been present.

(*g*) *Interaction.* Errors of this type are prevalent when a pre-measure changes the respondents' sensitivity to the independent variable(s). For example, a group of individuals may be given a questionnaire containing several attitude scales concerned with a particular brand or product category. These individuals are then likely to be particularly interested in, or sensitive to, advertisements and other activities involving these products.

(*h*) *Reactive errors.* Sometimes the artificial conditions of experimental situations or the behaviour of the experimenter produce consequences that change the nature of any effects caused by the treatment variable. For example, experiments designed to measure respondents' reactions to a range of visual stimuli under laboratory conditions may have little resemblance to reality where visual stimuli are noted amongst a myriad of other visual, auditory and olefactory distractions.

(*i*) *Measurement and timing.* Errors of this type arise when post-measurement is made at an inappropriate time to indicate the result of an experimental treatment. The outcome of advertising, for example, has a lagged repercussion. Care has to be taken where measuring advertising effectiveness to ensure that enough time has elapsed between the placing of the advertisement and the assessment of its consequence.

5. Experimental designs. The purpose of experimental designs is to try to remove the possibility of the errors mentioned in **4** above affecting an experiment. Unfortunately experimental designs cannot remove the last two sources of error (reactive errors and measurement timing) which can only be avoided by carefully designing the experiment itself.

Below is discussed a variety of experimental designs. The first group is termed *basic experimental designs* in which one treatment or independent variable only is manipulated. To aid understanding the following symbols will be used:

BM_n = before measurement: a measurement is made on the dependent variable prior to the introduction or manipulation of the independent variable.

AM_n = after measurement: a measurement made on the dependent variable after the introduction or manipulation of the independent variable.

E_n = experiment or treatment: the actual introduction or manipulation of the independent variable.

R_n = showing that the group is randomly selected and in the case of two or more groups being involved it denotes the particular group.

The choice of design will depend on cost factors and on the primary nature of experimental errors.

6. Basic experimental designs.

(*a*) "*After-only*" *design.*

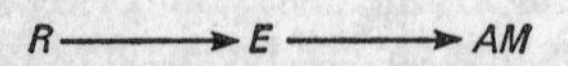

An experiment is conducted and an after-measure taken. A shop may place an advertisement in a local weekly newspaper to establish whether this may substantially increase sales. The shop has (from past sales) data on actual sales it would be likely to achieve without the advertisement. It attributes any difference in sales achieved in the experiment to advertising. "After only" designs are subject to a number of potential errors—the major one of which is "timelapse".

(*b*) "*Before-after*" *design.*

$$R \longrightarrow BM \longrightarrow E \longrightarrow AM$$

This incorporates a "before measure" and the experimenter is interested in the difference between the before and after measures, i.e. $AM - BM$. The design whilst giving data on conditions both before and during the experiment is still subject to experimental errors arising from—"timelapse", "maturation", "pretest", "instrumentation", "mortality" and "interaction".

(*c*) "*Simulated before-after*" *design.*

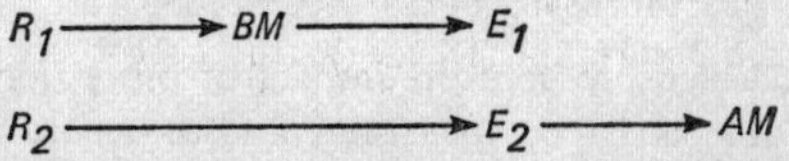

$$R_1 \longrightarrow BM \longrightarrow E_1$$

$$R_2 \longrightarrow E_2 \longrightarrow AM$$

This particular research design attempts to control for "premeasurement" and "interaction" by using separate groups of respondents for the "before" and the "after" measurement. Unfortunately, other factors remain as a source of experimental error—particularly "timelapse".

(*d*) "*Before-after with control*" *design.*

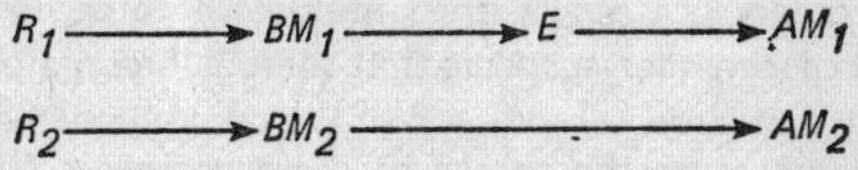

$$R_1 \longrightarrow BM_1 \longrightarrow E \longrightarrow AM_1$$

$$R_2 \longrightarrow BM_2 \longrightarrow AM_2$$

The addition of a control group R_2 effectively controls for errors due to "premeasurement", "maturation", "time lapse", "instrumentation" and "selection".

(*e*) "*After-only with control*" design.

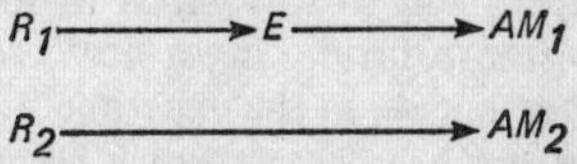

$$R_1 \longrightarrow E \longrightarrow AM_1$$

$$R_2 \longrightarrow AM_2$$

This design controls for all situations that the before-after control design does, except selection error, and it has the advantage of being cheaper.

(*f*) *"Four group" design.*

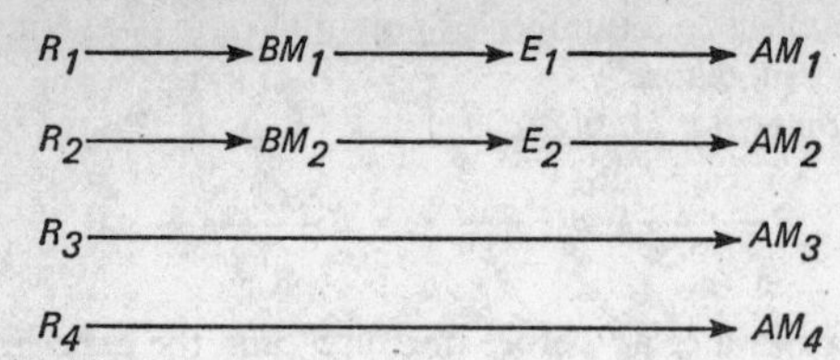

The design incorporates a before-after (with control) design and an after-only (with control) design. This is the most comprehensive design and it caters for all conditions except "measurement timing" and "reactive" error.

STATISTICAL DESIGNS

7. Statistical designs. Where the impact of more than one independent variable is to be measured and/or where specific extraneous variables are likely to confound results, a statistical design is desirable. There are three such designs which can be used to help implement marketing experiments.

(*a*) *Randomised blocks design.* These designs are founded on the assumption that the experimental groups are relatively similar on the dependent variable and that the members of these groups will react to the independent variable in a similar manner. Randomised blocks designs are suitable for those instances in which the experimenter suspects that there is one major external variable, such as total sales or sex of the respondents which may exert an influence on the results of the experiment. The fundamental idea of randomised blocks design is that the experimental units are "blocked" (i.e. grouped or stratified) according to the extraneous variable.

EXAMPLE: Suppose a researcher is faced with the problem of designing an experiment to test which of four points of sale display units to use in promoting a new product. Ninety-six stores agree to participate in the experiment, but it is felt that regional differences may affect customer reaction. The use of a randomised block design enables the problem to be circumvented. In this design, the units are stratified before treatments are allocated to the different test units (stores). In the illustration the random assignment of treatments is restricted to stores falling in a specific geographical area, e.g.

Randomised block design				
Northern stores	A	B	C	D
Midland stores	A	B	C	D
Southern stores	A	B	C	D

The blocks are three geographical locations (north, midlands, south). Assuming that blocks were of equal size, then 32 stores $\left(\frac{\text{total no. of shops}}{\text{geographical location}}\right)$ would be assigned to each block. Allocation of stores to blocks would not be found upon randomisation but according to their geographical location. The 32 stores within each block would then be randomly assigned to each of the four treatment levels (A, B, C or D), subject to the restriction that the four groups would be equal in size. The number of test units may be varied from block to block and treatment to treatment.

(*b*) *Latin square design.* This allows the researcher to control statistically for two non-interacting extraneous variables in addition to the independent variable. This is accomplished by employing a blocking technique similar to that described above. Each extraneous or blocking variable has to be divided into an equal number of blocks or levels. The independent variable must be divided into the same number of levels. The design format is that of a table with the rows representing the blocks on one extraneous variable and the columns representing the blocks on the other. The levels of the independent variable are then assigned to the cells in the table such that each level appears once only in each row and column.
e.g.

		Extraneous variable I: store type		
		Single Unit	*Co-operative*	*Supermarket chain*
Extraneous variable II: location	*Urban centre*	Price cut 2	Price cut 3	Price cut 1
	Suburbs	Price cut 1	Price cut 2	Price cut 3
	Rural area	Price cut 3	Price cut 1	Price cut 2

In the above example, store type and location of store are thought to be mutually independent extraneous variables which influence sales. The experimenter wishes to test for three levels of price cut. The design requires a minimum of as many stores as there are cells in the table (in this case 9). It should also be noted that the Latin square is so termed because there must always be as many rows as there are columns in the table.

(*c*) *Factorial design.* A factorial design is employed when it is required to measure the effect of two or more independent variables which might interact to produce results that neither could produce alone.

EXAMPLE: The problem is to determine the effect of varying coffee aroma in the jar and taste in the cup on customer preferences for a brand of coffee. A schematic presentation of the design is shown below:

COFFEE FACTORIAL DESIGN

		Taste in the cup			
		1	2	3	4
Aroma	1	a	b	c	d
in	2	e	f	g	h
the	3	i	j	k	l
jar	4	m	n	o	p

Sixteen different coffee formulations are prepared for the purposes of the experiment. These comprised all possible combinations of four different "tastes" and "aromas". Each variation is given to a different group of respondents and individuals are asked to rate the preparation on a five or seven point scale, where the scale maximum represents their "ideal" taste and aroma. The average score for the group is then computed for each group, i.e. each cell in the table, e.g.

		Taste			
		1	2	3	4
Aroma	1	1.7	1.6	3.6	4.4
	2	1.8	1.9	3.2	3.7
	3	1.9	1.8	3.1	3.4
	4	2.3	2.0	2.7	2.9

The combination in the top right-hand corner of the table with a mean score of 4.4 suggests that this particular blend is the highest rated of these presented in the experiment. Whilst this information is, of course, most useful it does illustrate one possible weakness of an experiment such as this; it does not enable the *ideal* combination to be isolated.

If, however, the numbers 1, 2, 3, 4 referred to different strengths of taste and aroma then it may very well be possible to determine statistically by analysis of variance (*see* XII) whether taste or aroma most affects respondents' reactions. Furthermore, by using more advanced statistical techniques (*see* XII) it may be possible to identify a more highly rated blend than the most favoured one in the experiment.

8. Summary. This chapter has examined the various types of research designs which may be employed in marketing experimentation to minimise the effect of a variety of sources of error. Methods of analysing the data generated from experiments which are dealt with in XII.

PROGRESS TEST 9

1. State all the likely sources of error that the following research designs do not eliminate:

(*a*) "before-after" design;
(*b*) "simulated before-after" design;
(*c*) "after only with control" design. **(4,6)**

2. Suggest an experimental design for each of the following:

(*a*) A researcher wishes to know which of two advertisements is likely to attract the most attention in a local newspaper.

(*b*) A washing powder manufacturer wishes to know what is the most satisfactory amount of shelf-space, height above the ground and positioning in the store, that should be bought relative to the "price schedule of a supermarket".

(*c*) A firm wishes to establish the combination of "sweetness" and "carbonation" of a new line of soft drinks which will be most preferred by the potential customers. **(6, 7)**

CHAPTER X

Data Acquisition—Secondary Sources within the U.K.

1. Introduction. This chapter describes the major sources of secondary data available for marketing research in Britain. It differentiates between internal and external sources of data and proceeds to examine the characteristics of each separately. Within the internal category is encompassed company records and trade association production statistics. External sources include government published data and other "public" sources, sources that are private within an industry and general sources such as the Press, directories, year-books and journals.

The sources mentioned are not intended to be a fully comprehensive list as that would be beyond the scope of this book. Instead, the aim is to highlight the major types of sources that can be beneficial in desk research.

2. Types of data. Data that is used in marketing research can be classified as either primary or secondary.

(*a*) *Primary data.* This is information that has been collected specifically in direct response to a problem that has arisen.

(*b*) *Secondary data.* Here the data already exists but it has not been collected especially for the investigation. This type of data is usually cheaper to obtain than primary data but it is likely to be more generalised in nature and less reliable.

This chapter discusses secondary data.

SOURCES OF SECONDARY DATA

3. Definition of secondary data. Secondary data for marketing research can be acquired from two types of sources; those which are available from within the organisation (internal sources) and those which can be obtained from outside the company (external sources).

4. Internal sources.

(*a*) *Nature of the data available from within the organisation.* It is strongly recommended on the grounds of ease of access and consequent savings in cost that the researcher begins an investigation by analysing the material available within the company. Frequently obtaining this information can present problems. There may be inter-departmental (and inter-divisional) hesitation to divulge apparently confidential records which could have repercussions on section managers. Sometimes department "empire building" encourages attempts to keep such statistics secret. The purpose of the study may be to obtain objective data to support hunches the instigator of the research has formed or ideas he has drawn from his knowledge of the market. In such projects the researcher may be expected to conjure up the data for his recommendations and conclusions from extraneous (and supposedly therefore unbiased) sources. Such expectations indicate that the users of the research are not co-operating fully with the investigator. In such cases, the research conducted will inevitably take longer to complete and may not be to such a high standard as could have been achieved with close collaboration.

Information obtained from within the company can be acquired with little cost. On the assumption that it is analysed systematically with full appreciation of biases, such information may provide the marketing researcher with a basis for more detailed study. Occasionally such data may suffice for the completion of the whole study.

5. Types of internal data.

(*a*) *Company records.* The data available within the company that are used for marketing research investigations include:

(*i*) *Sales statistics.* These can be analysed to show trends in product sales. The manner of collecting the data varies from company to company as does the depth of detail of the statistics obtained. For example, a company's sales may be divided into major product groups which could be assessed over given time periods (perhaps monthly, quarterly or annually). They could be further detailed by salesmen's territories, by the type of outlet though which the sales are effected, by size of order and so on. Customer complaints are also, on occasion, compared with sales. The quantity of data amassed may be such as to necessitate computer assistance. From all this data can be obtained not only sales trends and customer preferences but also, in some cases, comparisons which may indicate the more profitable product ranges, the effects of pricing policies etc. Market shares may be determined from an analysis of data from this source in conjunction with data from trade associations (*see* **5**(*b*)).

(*ii*) *Production records.* These can be used together with sales statistics to appraise stock levels and product delivery times.

(*iii*) *Financial accounts.* The analyses of company sales, gross margins and profits and losses by product group, by division and total company operations can provide helpful information. For example, it can illustrate those product groups with the highest gross margins that a company might wish to favour, or those with low margins whose operations might be examined in detail. When considering a low margin product group only recently introduced into the market, an increase in gross margins could be anticipated. Alternatively, a low margin product group could be at the end of its life cycle and there might be a case for deleting it from the product range altogether.

In many instances company accounts can be compared with total industry sales statistics available from trade associations and government published statistics. Nevertheless, care must be exercised to ensure that the statistics analysed are truly comparable since accountancy procedures differ between companies which give problems for interpretation.

(*iv*) *Employment statistics.* These may provide another indicator of the market situation. They can show the employment levels within different sectors of a firm and any significant increase or decrease will usually be directly related to market conditions.

(*b*) *Trade association production statistics.* Industry sales may be calculated from the statistics collected by trade associations through their members, yet before interpretation the composition of the records must be known. It is conceivable that the membership of the trade association does not encompass the whole industry, or that some members' activities overlap into other industries. Sometimes, a market leader does not join a trade association for fear of publicising confidential material or, because of its dominant position, the company does not feel the need to join. Alternatively, the membership may comprise only the leading firms and exclude a long tail of smaller firms. In consequence it is difficult to draw conclusions relating to all the firms in the market. Moreover, the members of a trade association may not always provide accurate returns of sales or production achieved and possibly the returns for the required period (usually on a monthly, quarterly or perhaps annual basis) are not readily available. Thus, at best the returns may only be estimates of true production levels. In some companies, company policy may advocate over (or under) statement of production levels, since if a company's sales are declining, it may be politic not to openly declare this to the other trade association members who are direct competitors. On occasion, a trade association may want to influence government policies (perhaps, regarding import restrictions) and consequently will publish statistics which, whilst not strictly incorrect, may distort the true situation.

Generally, trade association statistics are only available to members who have contributed to their compilation. However, once acquired, trade association statistics may be usefully analysed and can, if appropriately interpreted, provide an indication of a company's performance in comparison with competitors in the same market.

6. External sources.

(*a*) *Government published statistics*. These have a wide scope but vary in depth of coverage. The variation is largely related to the importance the government attaches to the statistics for administrative or political purposes. Thus, labour statistics concerning employees are collected in considerable depth (for example, weekly wage levels within different types of industry and for different categories of labour, absenteeism, regional differences etc.). This data is required and acquired in conjunction with the pay-as-you-earn method of tax collection. On the other hand, there is a dearth of statistics related to the earnings of self-employed persons who do not pay tax in the same way. Similarly, the detail of import and export statistics is proportional to Customs and Excise priorities. Product groups with low or negligible duties will often have less detailed statistics than those with high rates. Countries which have no trade tariffs between them will have considerably fewer trade statistics than those with complex, high tariffs and trade controls.

The government issues various publications that can help to identify the source of government statistics most appropriate to a particular problem. The comprehensive *Guide to Official Statistics* specifies the type of statistics that are published and where they may be found. *Government statistics—a brief guide to sources* is an annual, free publication issued by the Central Statistical Office which succinctly outlines many of the sources discussed in the much more detailed *Guide to Official Statistics*. The brief guide conveniently lists the addresses and telephone numbers of the government departments providing these statistics. The most up-to-date information concerning new developments in official statistics are published in the quarterly *Statistical News* and the weekly *Trade and Industry* journal. In some circumstances, it may be more appropriate to contact directly the Press and Information Service, Central Statistical Office, the Business Statistics Office or the relevant government department.

Government publications can be referred to at the Department of Trade's Statistics and Market Intelligence Library at Export House, 50 Ludgate Hill, London, EC4M 7HU. Many of the principal volumes are held by, or can be quickly obtained from, the major public libraries throughout the U.K.

SUMMARY OF GOVERNMENT PUBLISHED STATISTICS

The most frequently used statistics for marketing research purposes published by government departments include those concerned with general statistics, the economy, production, the retail industry, employment and overseas trade. These will now be outlined.

7. General statistics.

(*a*) *Monthly and annual digests*. These summarise a wide range of government statistics including movements of wages and salaries, consumer expenditure, energy consumption, production and consumption of main U.K. industries and an analysis by commodities of imports and exports.

(*b*) *Social trends*. This analyses key social and demographic statistics. It encompasses details of population, social groups, education, employment, health, housing, leisure, public safety, law enforcement etc.

8. The economy.

(*a*) *Economic trends.* This selection of tables and charts provides a summary of trends in the U.K. economy. The analysis is available for the U.K. and is further sub-divided to show local trends in England, Scotland, Wales and Northern Ireland.

(*b*) *Census of population.* Detailed statistics on population and households are collected in periodic censuses. From the data amassed special reports have been produced on immigration, economic activity, workplaces, transport to work and household composition. *Population trends* and *population projections* are made for the U.K. and its regions under the three groupings England and Wales, Scotland and Northern Ireland.

9. Production.

(*a*) *Production statistics.* These are produced annually in conjunction with the *Business Monitor* series of quarterly and monthly summaries of companies' own production statistics specified by industrial product.

(*b*) *Business Monitor series.* This is a detailed series of up-to-date production statistics which covers about 60 product groups.

(*c*) *Company finance business monitor* (*M*3). Statistics are given by industry concerning return on capital, dividends and interest as a percentage of assets, profits as a percentage of turnover etc.

(*d*) *Digest of U.K. energy statistics and energy trends.* These can provide helpful statistics on U.K. energy production and consumption. Further information can be obtained from the annual financial report for each of the relevant nationalised industries.

(*e*) *Other sources of production data.* Industries of particular interest to the government are well endowed with statistical data. Thus, in the building, construction and property sector there are the quarterly *Housing and Construction* statistics on output, orders, prices etc., sometimes detailed by region. *Ad hoc* statistical investigations are made to supplement the regular statistics and appear in the appendixes, an example being an analysis of high rise buildings. Statistics related to mining and quarrying, agriculture, fishing and food production are also collected in considerable detail.

(*f*) *National Economic Development Office* (*NEDO*) *publications.* These can be helpful sources for assessing development in industry. There are "Little Neddies" for 21 industries and all their reports are listed in *Nedo in Print* obtainable from NEDO Books, 1 Steel House, 11 Tothill Street, London, SW1H 9LJ.

10. Retail industry.

(*a*) *Census of distribution and other services.* The retail distribution trade is covered by a detailed census every ten years which is supplemented by a sample survey every five years. The census reports on retail businesses in terms of numbers, sizes, types, turnover, floor space, stocks, credit sales etc.

(*b*) *Retail trade, catering trades, cinemas report and motor trades.* These provide statistics on activities in the appropriate trade.

(*c*) *Family expenditure survey.* This annual survey details income and expenditure by type of household within the U.K. and includes some regional analyses.

(*d*) *General household survey.* Another useful source of family expenditure data is this continuous sample survey of households covering a wide range of social and socio-economic sectors of the community.

11. Employment. *The Department of Employment Gazette* gives (within different categories of employment) the latest statistics concerned with earnings, wage rates, overtime, unemployment, vacancies, hours of work, work stoppages due to industrial disputes, retail prices etc. Many of these statistics are available on a regional basis.

12. Overseas trade.

(*a*) *Overseas trade statistics of the U.K.* These provide detailed statistics of exports and imports by product group and by country collected on a monthly, quarterly and annual basis. The depth of detail is varied according to the trading countries and the product groups.

(*b*) *Overseas trade analysed in terms of industries.* This annual report is a summarised analysis of trade in major industry sectors. If more detail is desirable, the Bill of Entry service provided by Customs and Excise can be useful. The service can be tailored to the researcher's requirements to analyse most exports and imports under individual trade headings for individual countries over specific periods. A fee is charged to cover the costs of the service.

13. Other government statistics. Other departments issue statistics concerning such topics as taxation, transport, education, home affairs, justice and law, health and social services, overseas aid. Details of these are available from the relevant departments.

14. Other "public" sources.

(*a*) *Published financial accounts.* All registered companies must by law provide the Companies Registration Office (CRO) with details of their annual financial accounts and company reports. In addition, all companies operating in Scotland have to give their accounts to the Register of Companies, 102 George Street, Edinburgh 2. The Companies Act of 1976 obliges all public companies to submit annual accounts no later than seven months after their financial year ends and in the case of private companies within ten months.

CRO has to keep company files containing the company accounts available for public inspection. Companies House, City Road, London has had its major duties transferred to the purpose-built headquarters at Whitchurch Road, Cardiff. The company files have been progressively placed on micro-film so that anyone wishing to study information on a company now receives a microfiche film, which may be studied on any one of 320 viewing consoles in London or 30 in Cardiff. Alternatively, the microfiche can be sent to an inquirer. In the case of the Scottish Register of Companies, plans are being made to use microfilm but although these have not yet been put into effect there is one viewing console available for use with film issued through CRO in Edinburgh. However, microfiche for each company contains only three years of annual accounts and seven years of changes of directors, company secretaries and registered offices. Only the latest list of shareholders is shown.

CRO is re-introducing its postal inquiries service, whereby staff provide an inquirer with photocopies of company information. A drawback to this service is that particular details cannot be abstracted from company files. Another service, which at present costs a subscriber £120 per annum, is the Public Index which lists all companies by number and is available on microfiche, updated in total each month with daily additions and deletions.

The recent increase in the fee paid by a company to lodge an annual return (up from £3 to £20) should make firms more cautious about maintaining a company in existence that does not operate commercially. This will help to reduce the high numbers of ineffective companies, which should aid CRO administration.

Whilst company reports can provide a medium for analyses of competitor activity and even industrial trends or market size, they need to be treated with some degree of caution. For example:

(*i*) Accounting principles allow many alternative methods of accounting for the same situation. Thus, depreciation methods and the measuring of the cost of stock may vary.

(*ii*) Accounts treat a pound sterling (or whatever the monetary unit used) as a constant unit value. Thus, there is no need to provide for inflation or changes in the value of sterling in overseas markets, although many companies are now so doing.

(*iii*) The methods of assessing the value of assets is largely irrelevant in accountancy reporting. In the U.K. it is based on what was paid for the asset at an earlier date and makes no reference to current selling price of the asset, its current buying price or the discounted value of the expected marginal receipts. All of these methods of assessment, while more difficult to estimate, would have more relevance to management in their record of the ultimate profit and losses made.

(*b*) *Specialist agencies.* There are a number of companies in Britain supplying commercial intelligence which primarily involves company financial information and economic assessments. These include:

(*i*) *Dun and Bradstreet Ltd.* It gives credit ratings and capital structure analyses of both public and private companies worldwide. In Britain the *Register* covers about 200,000 firms in manufacturing and trading.

(*ii*) *Moodies Services Ltd.* Its services include individual company assessments obtained from published financial accounts and shown on cards.

(*iii*) *Exchange Telegraph Ltd.* (Extel). It provides a similar service to that given by Moodies. It is a financial abstracting service which gives subscribers a series of cards relating to about 1000 British quoted companies. The cards briefly show the names of directors, capital structure, financial tabulation of profit and loss over a period of up to ten years and an analysis of the balance sheet and management ratios for each company. A series of similar services cover unquoted companies.

15. Private sources within an industry.

(*a*) *Trade associations.* Most major industries, or service groups, have their own trade association which is capable of speaking to outside parties with one voice. Frequently, trade associations provide an information service for their members on matters pertaining to the industry which commonly includes trade statistics and technical advice. Secondary data provided by trade associations may in certain cases be considered an internal source of information for a company as discussed in **4**(*a*). Alternatively, it can be termed external source of information and as such is included in this section.

The *Directory of British Associations* is published annually by C.B.D. Research Ltd. and details some 8000 organisations, including trade associations, professional institutions, learned societies, trade unions, chambers of commerce, hobby societies etc., indexing them by fields of interest under about 3000 different headings.

(*b*) *Councils, committees and boards.* Another helpful publication issued by C.B.D. Research Ltd. is the *Directory of Councils, Committees and Boards.* This describes the functions and activities of both governmental and non-governmental boards, committees and other authorities, many of them concerned with specialised matters.

16. Press, journals, directories and yearbooks. Within the U.K., *The Financial Times*, *The Times*, *The Economist* and the *Investors' Chronicle* are among the leading newspapers and journals which comment on business and associated political and socio-economic activities. All publish surveys covering the major industries and regions in various levels of detail. They can give market forecasts and indicators which may be useful.

(*a*) *The Financial Times.* Its business information service uses the newspaper's library and staff resources to supply marketing data at a reasonable cost.

(*b*) *The Economist Intelligence Unit* (*E.I.U.*). This acts within the Economist group and issues regular reports specialising in major industries, for example, the motor industry or retail trade. The unit will undertake depth studies for clients.

(*c*) *Other publications.* There are numerous other publications used in marketing research including:

(*i*) *Kompass trade directory.* The British directory lists nearly

30 000 firms many of which are members of the C.B.I. and predominantly cover the manufacturing trades. There are two sectors of the directory, companies listed alphabetically within geographical regions and a detailed trade classification analysis.

(*ii*) *Kelly's directories*. The directory lists over 130 000 manufacturers, merchants, wholesalers and firms in the service industries. In one section firms are listed alphabetically with details of trade descriptions, address etc., and in the second section the companies are listed under 9000 classified trade headings.

(*iii*) *Who owns whom?* This publication has two lists—parent companies together with their associates and subsidiaries and, vice versa, associates or subsidiaries with their parent companies. There are also volumes which cover companies in the major European countries.

(*iv*) *Current British directories*. C.B.D. Research Ltd. issue this publication which gives a description of each of the 2500 directories listed in terms of information content, last date of publication, number of pages, price and publisher's name and address. The directories described include local directories published in the U.K., specialised directories of industries, trades, professions or individuals and yearbooks issued in the U.K. and the Commonwealth.

17. Miscellaneous sources. It is often worth approaching the following institutions for data which could be relevant to marketing research.

(*a*) *Banks*. Most of the commercial banks publish reviews of the economic climate and likely trends. Sometimes, studies are made and published concerning topics that could be significant for some marketing research investigations, for example, sources of housing finance.

(*b*) *National Institute of Economic and Social Research (N.I.E.S.R.)*. This institute reviews the economic climate in Britain. It issues quarterly analyses of the economic indicators and makes projections of likely trends in public borrowing and money supply, gross domestic product, personal disposable income, unemployment, consumer prices etc.

(*c*) *Association of special libraries and information bureau (ASLIB)*. If none of the above sources are able to provide the required data it is advisable to seek aid from ASLIB, 3 Belgrave Square, London, SW1X 8PL.

(*d*) *Professional associations.* In the U.K. there are two professional societies concerned with consumer and industrial marketing research. Each issues an annual list of its membership. Further, they have directories of specialist marketing research agencies which indicate the types of services each can offer.

(*i*) Market Research Society,
39 Hertford Street,
London, W1Y 8EP;

(*ii*) Industrial Marketing Research Association (IMRA),
11 Bird Street,
Lichfield,
Staffs, WS13 6PW;

(*iii*) Another professional body which has large library facilities and can be very useful is:

Institute of Marketing,
Moor Hall,
Cookham,
Berks, SL6 9HQ

SUMMARY

18. Summary. The types of sources of secondary data available within the U.K. for marketing research are varied. It is advised that the researcher begins by analysing the data that is to be obtained from the company's internal sources. These will be primarily company records which could be supplemented by trade association production statistics. The desk research might then turn to external sources starting with the government published statistics and marketing data. It could proceed to other public sources such as published financial accounts and the services offered by agencies specialising in the company financial assessments. Next, the researcher could consider sources which are available only to those operating in the particular industry that is to be examined. Press, journals, directories and year-books may also have to be consulted, together with miscellaneous published sources that could include bank publications. If, after all these sources have been consulted, suitable marketing data has not been found it is recommended that the library services of ASLIB are utilised. The professional marketing research associations may also be of assistance.

PROGRESS TEST 10

1. What are the two major types of data collected in marketing research? **(2)**

2. What are the types of secondary data that may be available from within a company to aid market assessments? **(4, 5)**

3. How far can external public sources supply a company with desk research material? **(6–14)**

4. In which ways can private sources within an industry serve the marketing researcher? **(15, 16)**

CHAPTER XI

Data Acquisition—Secondary Data—Sources of International Marketing Information

1. Introduction. This chapter shows some of the many sources of data available for international marketing desk research. It outlines the type of government help that can be obtained and the steps to be taken to procure overseas marketing data. It examines government published sources including trade statistics and development plans as well as trade and telephone directories. Sources of comparative data such as international organisations, specialised agencies, bank reports, and commercial specialist information research agencies are considered and sources of company information are detailed. Finally, other general sources are discussed including embassies and local chambers of commerce, newspapers and journals.

2. Sources of international marketing information.

(*a*) *Initial overseas marketing information guidance.* When international marketing is contemplated, it is advisable to approach the appropriate government body to obtain advice on methods of considering the problem and details of any financial help that may be available.

In Britain the British Overseas Trade Board (B.O.T.B.) directs the official government export promotion services. It consists of businessmen and representatives of the Department of Industry, the Foreign and Commonwealth Office and the Export Credits Guarantee Department. The Board's prime task is to ensure that the official export promotion activities are conducted with due regard to the needs of industry and commerce, whilst at the same time, using the available government export promotion resources to the best advantage.

The starting point is the examination of import and export trade statistics and country economic indicators which could include population data, gross domestic product assessments, production statistics, levels of employment and inflation rates. Directories of sources of such information have been compiled for the more developed countries and can give access to many potential data banks or likely informants.

Once this desk research material has been analysed, it may prove necessary to undertake a full-scale field survey and then trade and telephone directories can provide the basis for sample frames.

GOVERNMENT PUBLISHED SOURCES

3. Government published statistics.

(*a*) *Foreign trade statistics.* These are published by all countries showing imports and exports, usually in terms of the local currency (occasionally supplemented by volume units). However, these are not always, if ever, exactly comparable between countries. There is wide variation in recording systems, trade classifications differ and the quality of the statistics can be seriously affected at the collection stage by misdeclaration of goods, discrepancies in timing, in the valuation of goods and the standards of accuracy maintained. Further, many countries have long delays in the processing and publishing of the statistics.

(*i*) U.K. Customs and Excise trade statistics, although subject to criticisms from time to time, are among the more reliable government trade statistics especially when compared with those from countries which they can frequently be used to supplement. For example, in an examination of imports in the Oman, the export trade statistics of its major trading partners would probably give a more detailed and useful account than the import trade statistics of the Oman itself.

(*ii*) The day-to-day work related to export encouragement is handled by the staff of the Department of Industry in co-operation with Foreign and Commonwealth Office posts overseas. The export services and promotions division at Export House, London offers a range of export services to British exporters. These include market assessments, information on overseas tariffs and import regulations, help in organising business visits, advice in finding an agent or representative, some export marketing research (involving financial assistance in approved cases), market statistics, sales promotion assistance with overseas trade fairs and exhibitions, trade mission and so on. Two more especially helpful services provided are those of the following:

(*iii*) Export Credits Guarantee Department (E.C.G.D.) is a commercial business which acts as insurers to exporters against the risks of selling overseas.

(*iv*) Computerised Export Intelligence supplies exporters with details of export opportunities. The type of data given may be a request for tenders to install a new steel processing plant or details of a road building programme.

The Department of Industry publishes the weekly *Trade and Industry* journal which contains articles on export trends as well as features on the British market.

(*b*) *Method of procuring overseas data.* When investigating overseas markets the usual procedure is to begin with desk research aimed at determining the general economic climate and level of development achieved in the country to be examined. The investigation may then proceed to the more detailed published data that may be obtained from government sources, international organisations and international marketing research agencies.

4. Classification of trade statistics. The two most commonly used systems of categorising trade statistics are:

(*a*) *Standard Industrial Trade Classification (S.I.T.C.).* U.K. trading statistics are classified within the S.I.T.C., a coding system which involves a maximum of six numbers. As well as in Britain the system is used by many of her ex-colonies. Canada, however, has her own system which is more akin to that of U.S.A. than the U.K.

(*b*) *Brussels Trade Nomenclature (B.T.N.).* The other commonly used trade classification is the B.T.N. which defines the product by a code of up to eight numbers. It is favoured in trade statistics of most European countries and their spheres of influence.

5. Overseas published government statistics. Apart from foreign trade figures most governments issue statistics which record economic indicators. They can encompass some, or all, of the types published by the British government in greater or less detail (*see* X). The most commonly produced statistics are those related to production outputs by major industries (primary and secondary), employment levels, inflation indicators such as the retail price index, house building starts, population trends etc. The range and quality of the statistics vary greatly, reflecting the importance of the statistics to each particular country.

6. Development plans. These are produced by most of the underdeveloped nations and some of the more developed countries. They can provide substantial historical data such as past growth rates of the gross national product, population, levels of inflation or house construction increases on which forecasts can be made. The standards of these plans differ widely. They frequently indicate the optimistic development that long-term government planning is anticipating and the ultimate implementation is not likely to be precisely in accord with the plan. Occasionally the plans are little more than propaganda and are almost worthless. However, in many instances, development plans are extremely useful, especially as an indicator of a country's economic climate. They can give potential large scale development intentions and although the exact timing of the implementation of the plan may not be accurate, knowledge of these intentions will help international marketing decisions. Thus, if a company in Britain appreciates that in another country there are plans to improve the infrastructure or proposals for a new steel plant or the expansion of the docks, then the company can prepare long-term plans, probably in conjunction with the B.O.T.B. export promotional services, for possible business at some date in the future.

7. Overseas trade and telephone directories. These are another widely used source of information but, as with all overseas data, their reliability, accuracy and depth of detail will differ from country to country and from trade to trade. Nevertheless, they can be helpful in determining the major manufacturers or users of specific products and they can be used, with care, for the preparation of sampling frames.

SOURCES OF COMPARATIVE DATA

8. International organisations. There is a *Yearbook of International Organisations* published by the Union of International Associations, Brussels which contains many of the sources of comparative data.

Some of the major organisations that publish comparative statistical data are:

(*a*) *United Nations*. The *U.N. Statistical Yearbook* gives by country population, rates of growth of population, gross domestic product, national income statistics etc. However, although the data covers most countries in the world, it does for that same reason tend to be dated by the time it is published.

The United Nations issues other comparative statistics such as:

(*i*) U.N. annual bulletin of housing and building statistics for Europe.

(*ii*) U.N. quarterly bulletin of steel statistics for Europe.

These types of publications can be a useful aid to inter-country comparisons.

(*b*) *European Economic Community* (*E.E.C.*). The statistics office of the European Community (EUROSTAT) has the principal aim of providing statistical data required for formulating and monitoring community policies. EUROSTAT is organised into six main directorates which cover statistical methodology and information processing; general statistics and national accounts; social and demographic statistics; agriculture, forestry and fisheries; energy, industry and handicrafts; trade, transport and services. Whilst it is advisable to consult EUROSTAT for any data that may be available and although inter-country comparisons are produced, the statistics from EUROSTAT still lack detail. Doubtless, in time, this deficiency will be remedied.

(*c*) *European Free Trade Association* (*EFTA*). This publishes statistics which compare its member countries on economic and social criteria. The member countries are Austria, Britain, Denmark, Finland, Iceland, Norway, Portugal, Sweden and Switzerland.

(*d*) *Organisation for Economic Co-operation and Development* (*O.E.C.D.*). This has twenty-four member nations from the developed world including European countries, U.S.A., Japan, Canada, Australia and New Zealand. The O.E.C.D. has two particularly useful series of publications:

(*i*) *Main economic indicators*. This is a monthly statistical comparison of O.E.C.D. countries' economic activity in terms of rates of inflation, cost of living indices, employment levels, wages by broad type of industry and, sometimes, statistics on house building.

(*ii*) *Economic surveys*. These are produced every few years on particular countries and, apart from economic statistical data, they provide an analysis of government financial policies and the progress of the major industries in the country concerned. Countries covered in this series include Austria, Denmark, Finland, Iceland, Norway, Sweden and Switzerland.

(*e*) *Other international organisations*. Those which can be approached for country statistical data include:

(*i*) UNESCO;

(*ii*) U.N. General Agreement on Tariffs and Trade (GATT);

(*iii*) U.N. economic commission for Europe, Asia, Africa and Latin America;

(*iv*) International Monetary Fund (I.M.F.);

(*v*) International Bank for Reconstruction and Development (I.B.R.D.).

9. Specialised agencies. These can frequently provide international comparative data in their own appropriate spheres.

(*a*) *Food and Agricultural Organisation* (*F.A.O.*). This supplies statistics of population growth and food production levels. It makes projections of future demands for most underdeveloped countries.

(*b*) *Other specialised agencies*. These include:

(*i*) International Labour Organisation (I.L.O.);

(*ii*) International Union of Official Travel Organisations;

(*iii*) International Air Transport Association (I.A.T.A.);

(*iv*) International Civil Aviation Organisation (I.C.A.O.).

10. Bank reports.

(*a*) *World Bank*. This authority makes world-wide inter-country comparisons of economic activity. Its publications include:

(*i*) *The World Bank Atlas*. This gives data on population and gross national product *per capita* together with growth rates for each country.

(*ii*) *Trends in developing countries*. This shows world-wide trends in population, economic growth, international capital flow and international trade.

(*iii*) *World Bank catalogue*. This highlights recent studies conducted by the Bank in developing countries.

(*b*) *Other bank reports*. Many banks provide detailed individual country reports, whereas others concentrate on the analysis of economic trends on a world-wide basis. Some publications produced by the banks which can be helpful for the assessment of economic activity in international markets are:

(*i*) Lloyds Bank country economic reports;
(*ii*) Midland Bank spotlight on overseas trade;
(*iii*) Bank of London and South America (BOLSA) review;
(*iv*) Grindlays Bank review.

11. Commercial specialist information research agencies. There are various directories of published market research which may help the researcher to obtain desk research material. They can also indicate which marketing research agencies have the expertise required to complete a specific marketing research assignment.

(*a*) *The B.O.T.B. International directory of published research.* This directory contains over 4000 study summaries completed since 1973 by more than 400 leading marketing research firms. The coverage is world-wide.

(*b*) *The European directory of market research surveys.* This publication, edited by Thomas Landau, gives data on about 1500 market research surveys prepared in Europe in both consumer and industrial markets since 1972. It is divided into two parts, the first provides a checklist of the subjects and countries covered, and the second a complete directory listing of surveys.

(*c*) *Published data on European industrial markets.* This is a two-part directory issued by Industrial Aids Ltd. The first part is a guide list of over 1000 market studies, whereas the second covers a wide range of other sources of published data.

(*d*) *U.S. and Canadian marketing surveys and services.* This lists about 1500 multiclient marketing reports and syndicated continuing services in North America. The 125 consulting firms listed include both industrial and consumer marketing research companies.

(*e*) *C.B.D. Research Ltd. guides to directories and associations.* This company produces some extremely useful guides to sources. Apart from those related to British sources, there are the *Current European directories*, the *Current African directories* and the *Directory of European associations. The European companies: a guide to sources of information* gives data on the sources available in each country in Europe.

(*f*) *Economist Intelligence Unit* (*E.I.U.*). This group publishes quarterly economic reviews and annual supplements which cover about 80 countries in detail including Iran, Saudi Arabia, Jordan, Brazil and Malaysia. These reviews show the economic indicator and discuss in some depth market trends in each country. The E.I.U. offers consultancy services for the countries in which it specialises.

12. Choice of marketing research agency. There are two directories of marketing research agencies that can help to evaluate the most suitable choice for an international marketing investigation.

(*a*) *The International directory of market research organisations.* This is published by the Market Research Society and covers about 500 market research organisations in 48 countries.

(*b*) *European guide to industrial marketing consultancy.* This is an Industrial Marketing Research Association (IMRA) publication. It details about 120 consultancies and their subsidiaries operating in Britain and Europe.

13. Sources of company information. The most reliable sources of company information are company annual reports, Stock Exchange year-books, press commentary, stockbrokers' reports and bank advice, the standards of which vary considerably. These all originate within the country in which the company operates.

14. Specialist agencies for company assessments. When a company's background is to be examined, it is often advisable to consult a credit assessment company. In Britain some of the agents offering these services for overseas companies are:

(*a*) *Dun and Bradstreet Ltd.* This firm can provide appraisal of major international and national companies and produces an international market guide to Europe among its many services. This guide has full names and addresses, precise details of lines of business and their own credit worthiness estimate of 320 000 businesses in 19 continental European countries. Dun and Bradstreet Ltd. have associates in many countries to help in company appraisals.

(*b*) *Exchange Telegraph Ltd. (EXTEL).* This is a company financial abstracting service which supplies data on the larger European, Australian and North American companies. It is not as extensive as the Dun and Bradstreet Ltd. coverage.

(c) *Jane's Major Companies in Europe*. This covers the finances of about 1100 European companies in finance, services, light industry, industrial chemicals, engineering, building, metals and minerals.

(d) *Kompass*. This directory of industry, trade and services gives company data which include capital, number employed, names of one or more directors, list of activities etç. Directories exist for the European and Scandinavian countries, Australia, Hong Kong, Indonesia, Japan, Morocco, Singapore, Taiwan and Thailand.

(e) *Information Internationales*. This covers 800 of the largest companies in Europe, North America and Japan. It gives a detailed account of each company's activities, financial accounts, subsidiaries, affiliates and associated companies.

(f) *McCarthy Information Ltd*. This company provides a news abstracting service covering leading newspapers and periodicals in Europe as well as the British press.

OTHER GENERAL SOURCES OF DATA

15. Embassies and local chambers of commerce. The local embassy of the country concerned in the investigation can sometimes be helpful in providing local commentary. However, it must be appreciated that embassies are more interested in the promotion of their own exporters than in encouragement of imports to their own countries.

Local chambers of commerce maintain general business directories and data on local companies. The statistics collected are usually limited.

16. Newspapers and journals. Newspapers publish articles and surveys concerning overseas countries and their markets from time to time. The standard of the coverage varies widely but the newspaper most geared to the provision of this type of service in Britain is *The Financial Times*. There are numerous other journals which comment on overseas markets, some specialise entirely in foreign trade and others give occasional surveys of particular relevance to international marketing. Over all, the most helpful publications are as follows:

(a) *The Financial Times*. It gives detailed individual country surveys which assess the economic climate and political stability, as well as analysing trends in the country's major industries. *The Financial Times* also publishes product surveys on a world-wide front and in its commercial capacity it reports on trends in international trade. Further, it has a business information service which enables subscribers to benefit from the Financial Times library and staff expertise.

(*b*) *Foreign economic trends*. This highlights key economic indicators for each country and can aid inter-country comparisons.

(*c*) *Business Europe*. This issues an annual table of indicators of market size for about 80 countries in four continental groups, Western and Eastern Europe, Africa and the Middle East.

(*d*) *Investors' Chronicle*. Supplements on overseas countries are published from time to time.

(*e*) *Predicast World Forecasts*. This publication series is worth considering for quick broad-brush analysis of world trend forecasts. It covers countries within continents and gives forecasts of economic indicators made by such varied sources as government planning authorities, international organisations and trade journals. The more frequently listed indicators are growth rates for population, gross national product, rates of inflation, house construction and major industries' production. The sources of the forecasts are indicated.

(*f*) *Concise guide to international markets*. This is published by arrangement with the U.K. Charter of the International Advertising Association and provides data on marketing and advertising statistics in 110 world markets. The data includes population, literacy, languages, religions, main towns, retail and wholesale structure, details of advertising agencies and controls, media expenditure and market research facilities.

17. Summary. There is a wide range of sources of data available for desk research into international markets. However, the standards and reliability of the data vary greatly. The marketing researcher is advised to investigate the help that government services can give and to consult government published sources which may provide indicators of market size and trends. These sources can include government statistics (both those produced by Britain and those by overseas countries), development plans, trade and telephone directories. Comparative statistical data is available from numerous international organisations and specialised agencies. If required, commercial specialist information agencies can produce specific data on certain companies and markets. Other general sources of data worth considering are press and journal commentary.

PROGRESS TEST 11

1. How does the government encourage international marketing? **(2, 3)**
2. Distinguish between the two commonly used systems of classification of trade statistics. **(4)**
3. In which ways can development plans be used in marketing research? **(6)**
4. What are the major sources of international comparative data? **(8, 9, 10)**
5. How can the marketing researcher obtain information on companies operating in an overseas country? **(13, 14, 15)**

PART FOUR

DATA ANALYSIS AND INTERPRETATION

CHAPTER XII

Data Analysis

1. Introduction. This chapter examines a variety of statistical techniques which are available to analyse data. Examples of the most frequently used techniques are shown in simplest form, or, alternatively, the principles of the method are described. Where techniques involve complex mathematics, interested readers are recommended to consult a variety of text books which will provide them with more information. The use of computer packages is advised when carrying out most of the techniques discussed in this chapter. Invariably, either the mathematics or the quantity of data will make it difficult to carry out such analyses by hand. In particular the S.P.S.S. (Statistical Packages for the Social Sciences) system is advocated and readers are advised to consult the S.P.S.S. manual (*see* Bibliography).

Choice of appropriate technique depends on three factors:

(*a*) Whether or not the data can be partitioned into criterion (dependent) and predictor (independent) variables.

(*b*) Whether the data is nominal, ordinal or interval/ratio scaled.

(*c*) The number of criterion (dependent) and predictor (independent) variables considered.

Each of these points will be discussed in some detail, but it should be noted that there are a large variety of statistical methods and only the more commonly used ones are discussed in detail. In Appendix I a list will be found of a full range of techniques together with the instances when each one might be applied.

Further information on all the techniques may be obtained from the references cited in the reading list.

2. Partitioned and non-partitioned data. It is often possible to hypothesise that a relationship exists between one variable and another, or, between one set of variables and another set. Sales, for example, may be associated with advertising, pricing, product and distribution strategies. In such cases, it is possible to partition the data into predictor and criterion variables. Under these circumstances statistical tests of significance such as the *t*-test, chi-square test and *Z*-test may be used to test for associations. Alternatively, correlation techniques or analysis of variance may be used. The choice of the appropriate technique depends on how the data is scaled and the number of variables involved.

There may be occasions when no particular variable can be singled out as a "criterion" or "dependent" variable. Under such circumstances the objective of analysis may well be:

(*a*) To find a way to group people into distinctly different groups which exist in a larger population, for example, ascertaining the extent to which segments of households exist whose purchasing habits are distinctly different from those of another segment.

(*b*) To find a set of dimensions that are latent in a set of variables, for example, underlying attitudes towards a product from a multitude of attitude statements.

In these situations "factor analysis" and "cluster analysis" are powerful techniques which can be employed to accomplish these objectives. The mathematics required to conduct a factor analysis or a cluster analysis is complex. Interested readers are advised to consult the texts mentioned in the Bibliography. It should also be noted that there is a standard S.P.S.S. computer package which will perform factor analysis.

3. S.P.S.S. computer packages. There is now a large variety of computer packages available. The whole idea of computer packages is to simplify the task of preparing data and writing computer programmes, so that any person can teach himself to use a computer to solve complex problems. Readers are advised to consult the S.P.S.S. Primer manual before consulting the S.P.S.S. manual itself.

4. Interval or ratio scaled data. Most of the commonplace statistical techniques of analysis found in textbooks on statistics refer specifically to those instances where both criterion and predictor variables are interval or ratio scaled. Choice of an appropriate technique to analyse data or test a hypothesis depends on the number of criterion and predictor variables and the exact nature of the problem. In the following sections, attention will be focused upon a number of problems in which the data is interval or ratio scaled and will describe the appropriate method of analysis to adopt.

INTERVAL OR RATIO SCALED DATA

5. Applications of the Z and t-test to the testing of hypotheses. In III these two statistics were discussed in the context of statistical estimation. Here they will be considered as a means of testing hypotheses. The *Z*-test can be used to assess whether two means or two proportions differ from one another statistically.

EXAMPLE: A researcher is trying to establish whether, as a result of a specific advertising campaign, brand awareness has been increased. Prior to the advertising campaign 73 per cent of 1000 respondents to a sample survey could not recall the product's brand name, whereas after the experiment in a second sample of 1000 respondents only 45 per cent could not recall the brand name. Both samples were randomly selected and mutually exclusive.

SOLUTION: Apply the *Z*-test to test for a significant difference between the two proportions. From the formula:

$$Z = \frac{p_1 - p_2}{\left(\frac{p_1 q_1}{n_1} + \frac{p_2 q_2}{n_2}\right)^{\frac{1}{2}}}$$

where $p_1 =$ proportion in the first sample not recalling the brand name;

$p_2 =$ proportion in the second sample not recalling the brand name;

$q_1 = 1 - p_1$;

$q_2 = 1 - p_2$.

By substitution in the example:

$$Z = \frac{0.73 - 0.45}{\left(\frac{0.73 \times 0.27}{1000} + \frac{0.45 \times 0.55}{1000}\right)^{\frac{1}{2}}}$$

$$= 13.3$$

The figure of 13.3 is much larger than even the Z-statistic of 2.58 which indicates that one can be 99 per cent certain that there has been a significant change. It should be concluded therefore that the change is highly significant.

The example illustrates the use of testing for the significance between proportions in uncorrelated large samples. The references quoted in the reading list give further examples, i.e. for the difference between means (large and small samples) and the difference between proportions (small samples).

Choice of test depends upon sample size and whether or not the two sets of data are correlated.

6. Correlation and regression methods. There are four basic techniques:

(*a*) pearson product-moment correlation;
(*b*) bivariate regression;
(*c*) multiple regression;
(*d*) canonical correlation.

The first three of these ((*a*), (*b*) and (*c*)) are readily understood and interpreted. Canonical correlation is the most difficult to comprehend and it deals with the case where there are multiple criterion variables and multiple predictor variables. (Readers interested in this latter method are advised to consult the references shown in the Bibliography. It is worthwhile to note that there is a standard S.P.S.S. package available which will perform a canonical correlation.) The other three techniques are discussed below.

(*a*) *Pearson product-moment correlation.* Sometimes, it is necessary to find the strength of a relationship between two variables. The marketing researcher may wish to assess how shelf space is related to sales of a product in a supermarket. Suppose the supermarket keeps records of the amount of shelf space it has given to the product in the past and also the weekly sales volume of the product. The following data is held:

Week	*Shelf space* (m^2)	*Sales volume* (*units*)
1	4.8	827
2	6.2	1046
3	11.2	1474
4	5.8	1037
5	7.4	1146
6	7.6	1018
7	5.8	934
8	11.0	1248
9	5.8	1046
10	6.4	1027

The extent of the association can be calculated by using the "coefficient of correlation". This statistic calculates a number between −1.00 and +1.00 which indicates the degree of association between the two variables. The number may be interpreted as follows:

+1.00 strong positive association
+0.50 positive association
0.00 no correlation
−0.50 negative association
−1.00 strong negative association

If the relationship can be shown to be positive, it can be assumed that as the amount of shelf space increases so does sales volume. If the relationship is negative then as the amount of shelf space increases sales will decrease. The coefficient is calculated by applying the following forumula:

$$r = \frac{N\Sigma XY - (\Sigma X)(\Sigma Y)}{((N\Sigma X^2 - (\Sigma X)^2)(N\Sigma Y^2 - (\Sigma Y)^2))^{\frac{1}{2}}}$$

where r = coefficient of correlation;
N = number of observations;

and X and Y are raw data observations.

In the example above it can be shown that $r = +0.91$. This suggests that there is a strong positive association between shelf space and sales, in other words shelf space and sales are likely to be closely related.

(*b*) *Bivariate regression.* It might be useful for the firm to know what sales would be achieved if it were to alter the display space available to the product involved. For example, if the shop were to give over 20 m^2 of shelf space to the product. It should be emphasised that, because two variables are correlated significantly, one cannot assume that there is a cause and effect relationship present. However, if one can develop a logical argument that a cause and effect relationship might exist and then find correlation evidence to support this argument, then it could be assumed that such a relationship exists. To establish the nature of this relationship the technique of bivariate regression can be used. The relationship between the two variables above can be shown graphically (*see* Fig. 5).

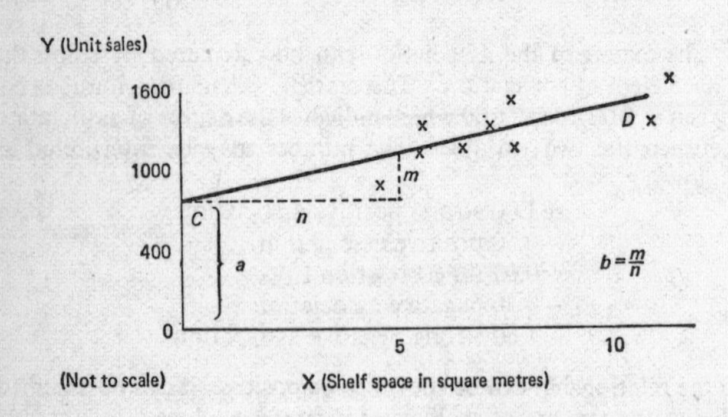

FIG. 5 *Graphical representation of the relationship between sales (Y) and shelf space (X).*

The line of best fit to the data (*CD*) is termed the least squares regression line. The idea of regression analysis is to express the relationship between two variables in the form of an equation such that:

$$Y = a + b\ X \text{ (see Fig. 5)}$$

where a is the distance between the origin (O) of the graph and C (on the vertical axis), this is termed the Y intercept value. The slope of the line with respect to the horizontal (X) axis is represented by b (the ratio $\frac{m}{n}$).

As will be realised from trying to read an equation from a graph, or even trying to find the line of best fit by hand, it is at best a hazardous way of tackling the problem. Fortunately, a and

b can be estimated mathematically by using the following equations:

$$b = \frac{\Sigma XY - ((\Sigma X)(\Sigma Y)/N)}{\Sigma X^2 - ((\Sigma X)^2/N)}$$

and $$a = \bar{Y} - b\bar{X}$$

In the example illustrated above it can be calculated that:

$$b = 72.8 \text{ and } a = 556$$

Hence it can be predicted that if shelf space were to be increased to 20 m², sales might amount to 2012 units (mean estimate), i.e.

$$\text{Sales} = 556 + (20 \times 72.8) = 2012 \text{ units}$$

NOTE: This is a mean estimate only—the standard error of the estimate needs to be considered and a confidence interval specified (*see* III).

The standard error of the estimate is found by the formula:

$$s\,YX = sY\,(1 - r^2XY)^{\frac{1}{2}}(n/n-2)^{\frac{1}{2}}$$

where sYX = the standard error of the estimate of Y from X;
sY = the standard deviation of Y;
r^2XY = the correlation between Y and X all squared;
n = the sample size.

$$s\,YX = 177\,(1-(0.91)^2)^{\frac{1}{2}}(10/8)$$
$$= 82.1 \text{ or approximately 82 units}$$

Hence the 95 per cent confidence level estimate of sales that will be generated with 200 m² of shelf space is:

2012	±	1.96	×	82.1
(mean estimate)		(*Z*-value for 95 per cent *cl*)		(standard error of the estimate)

or between 1851 and 2173 units

(*c*) *Multiple regression analysis.* The technique enables quantitative evidence to be found to support the view that behaviour in one variable (the criterion variable) can be associated with a corresponding set of behaviour patterns exhibited by a number of other variables (the predictor variables) in conjunction with one another. The nature of the association is expressed in terms of a linear equation, thus:

$$Y = a_0 + b_1X_1 + b_2X_2 + \ldots b_nX_n + u$$

where Y = the criterion variable;
$X_{i \ldots n}$ = the predictor variables;
b_n = parametric subscripts;
a_0 = a constant;
u = an error term.

EXAMPLE: Ice cream sales (Y) at a resort are thought to be associated with the mean monthly temperature in degrees centigrade at noon (X_1), the number of visitors to a resort (X_2), the number of centimetres of monthly rainfall (X_3) and there is also a small proportion (u) for which, as yet, no association has been found. The ideas can best be grasped from studying Fig. 6.

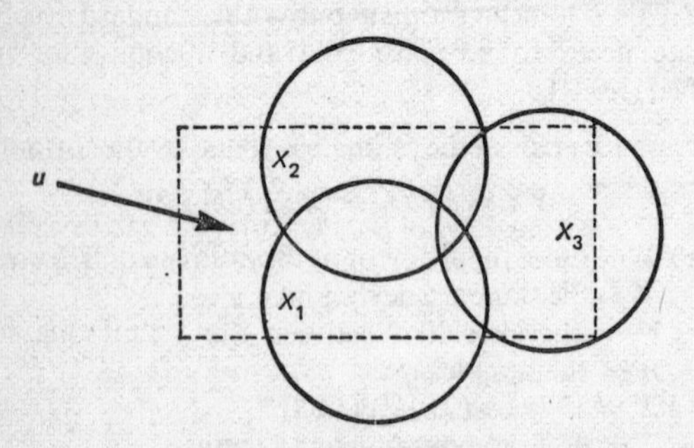

FIG. 6 *The basic idea behind multiple regression analysis.*

The area within the rectangle represents sales of ice cream over a period of time and the area within each of the circles represents each of the three independent variables discussed above. The extent to which each of the independent variables is associated with the sales of ice cream is represented by the degree of overlap between each circle and the rectangle. It will be noted that the circles do in fact overlap each other, as well as the rectangle, and that one part of the rectangle is not overlapped at all.

The residual error in the equation is represented by u. That is the variation in sales that cannot be associated with any of the independent variables. The area within the rectangle, where two or more circles overlap, shows the proportion of variance in the sales of ice-cream which is associated with variance in two or more of the independent variables.

Ideally, for an equation to have high predictive ability the residual error (u) needs to be minimal. The larger the value and variance of u, the less useful the equation will be in predicting values for the criterion variable.

ORDINAL AND NOMINAL SCALED DATA

7. Ordinal scaled data. A different set of techniques may have to be employed to analyse data consisting of ordinal values. If the data comprises a mixture of "ordinal" and "ratio/interval" scaled values then the usual approach is to transform the ordinal data into interval scaled data. A satisfactory method of transforming data is shown in VI).

Where all the data is ordinal scaled or there is a mixture of ordinal and nominal scaled values, a different set of methods of data analysis is necessary (*see* Appendix I for details).

The best known method of testing to see if a relationship exists between two sets of ordinal data is the Spearman rank correlation coefficient.

8. Nominal scaled values. As is the case with ordinal scaled values it is possible to transform nominal scaled data into interval scaled values. The transformation takes the form of creating what are termed dummy variables (*see* VI). Once nominal scaled data has been transformed into dummy variables it can be treated as if it were interval scaled.

A number of techniques have been developed to analyse data which has nominal values or where there is a mixture of ordinal and nominal scaled data, i.e. without any transformation of the data into interval scaled values. Two of these techniques are discussed below and reference to the other methods will be found in Appendix I.

(*a*) *Chi-square in conjunction with contingency tables.* There is an S.P.S.S. package which will perform this kind of analysis. The technique is applied in those instances where there is a single nominal scaled criterion variable and one or more nominally scaled predictor variables.

EXAMPLE: A firm is trying to establish whether there is any significant difference between the "social class" classification of people and whether or not those people seek further information about a particular advertising message. 1000 respondents were interviewed and the following results obtained:

	Social classification of people:		
	Working class and those of the lowest subsistence level	*Lower middle and skilled working classes*	*Upper middle and middle classes*
Behaviour			
Information sought	93	172	186
Information not sought	183	112	58

(196 respondents did not see or hear the message.)

If there were no significant differences between social classes in respect of requests for further information then it would be expected that each social class would show the average rate of requests for further information. It can be seen that a total of 451 out of 804 of the respondents sought information—an average of 56 per cent. Amongst "working class and those of lowest subsistence level", it would be expected that 56 per cent of the total in this group—total = 276—or 155 would seek further information. The figures shown in brackets in each and every cell of the "contingency table" below denote the expected results:

	Working class etc.	*Lower middle class etc.*	*Upper middle class etc.*	*Total*	%
Information sought	93 (155)	172 (159)	186 (137)	451	56
Information not sought	183 (121)	112 (125)	58 (107)	353	44
Total	276	284	244	804	100

The formula for the chi-square test of significance is:

$$\text{chi-square} = \text{sum of } \frac{(\text{actual}-\text{expected value})^2}{\text{expected value}}$$

$$\text{or } \sum_{1=i}^{h} \frac{(0_i - E_i)^2}{E_i}$$

where 0_i = an individual observed value;
E_i = an individual expected value.

By arithmetic this value is computed to be 98.95. To interpret the chi-square it is necessary to know the degree of freedom (*see* III, 9). To find the degrees of freedom in a contingency table, the first row and column in the table are eliminated and the remaining cells represent the number of degrees of freedom in the table. In this case, degrees of freedom are two.

Next, reference is made to the table in Appendix IV. Assuming that it is desired to be 99 per cent confident that there is a significant difference present in the table, the value opposite 2 degrees of freedom is read off under the column headed 0.99. In this case, it is 9.21 and since the value obtained above far exceeds this value it should be concluded that the difference did not come about by chance. In other words, requests for information appear to vary with the social class of the person.

(*b*) *Analysis of variance*. This form of analysis is recommended when there is a single ordinal or interval/ratio scaled criterion variable and multiple nominal scaled predictor variables. There is an S.P.S.S. package available to facilitate the use of this method of analysis.

EXAMPLE: A brand manager has arranged to show the prototype of a new washing machine to a dozen key dealers. He is undecided between which of three special features to add to the washing machine and takes the opportunity to ask the dealers for their opinions. As an aid to his decision making, he asks the dealers to rate each of the special features on a ten point scale. The following results were obtained:

	Feature			
	A	B	C	Total
Dealer				
1	10	7	3	20
2	6	5	9	20
3	9	8	5	22
4	8	10	9	27
5	10	7	4	21
6	7	10	2	19
7	6	8	8	22
8	8	10	3	21
9	9	7	5	21
10	10	5	2	17
11	7	2	5	14
12	5	6	8	19
Total	95	85	63	243

Now, the brand manager wants to know:

(*a*) that the dealers discriminate between the special features;

(*b*) that the dealer ratings are reliable (they do not differ significantly amongst themselves).

The analysis of variance proceeds as follows:

(*a*) Calculate the "total sum of squares":

$$SS_t = \Sigma X^2 - \frac{(\Sigma X)^2}{N} \quad \text{(N is the number of cells in the table.)}$$

$$= (10^2+7^2+3^2+\ldots+6^2+8^2) - \frac{(243)^2}{36}$$

$$= 1857 - 1640.25$$

$$= 216.75$$

(*b*) Calculate the sum of squares for the rows, dealers:

$$SS_r = \frac{(20^2+20^2+22^2+27^2+\ldots+14^2+19^2)}{3} - \frac{(243)^2}{36}$$

$$= 1675.66 - 1640.25$$

$$= 35.41$$

(*c*) Calculate the sum of squares for the columns, features:

$$SS_c = \frac{(95^2+85^2+63^2)}{12} - \frac{(243)^2}{36}$$

$$= 1684.92 - 1640.25$$

$$= 44.67$$

(*d*) Calculate the "residual error sum of squares". This error term is a combination of interaction and error effects.

$$SS_e = SS_t - (SS_r + SS_c)$$
$$= 216.75 - (35.41 + 44.67)$$
$$= 136.67$$

NOTE: The *total* sum of squares is obtained by specifically squaring the deviation of each score from the mean of *all* 36 scores. The sum of squares for columns and rows is specifically found by taking the mean for rows or columns, getting its deviation from the *total* mean, squaring this deviation, and then multiplying each of these by the number of individuals in each group (n). The formulae used in (*a*), (*b*) and (*c*) effectively produce the same results.

Finally a table is set up:

Source of the variation	*Degrees of freedom* ($n-1$)	*Sum of squares*	*Mean square* (SS/df)	*F ratio*
Rows (dealers)	11	35.41	3.2	0.52
Columns (features)	2	44.67	22.3	3.60
Error	22	136.67	6.2	—
Total	35	216.75	—	—

NOTE: The *F*-ratio is determined in each case by dividing the mean square of the rows or the columns by the mean square of the error.

The *F*-ratio for the rows is not found to be significant at the 5 per cent level. With 11 and 22 degrees of freedom, a value of greater than 2.26 would have been required. The brand manager might therefore conclude that the dealers' estimates are reliable. The *F*-ratio for the columns is found to be significant at the 5 per cent level. With 2 and 22 degrees of freedom, a value of 3.44 or greater has to be obtained for the ratio to be significant. The brand manager might therefore conclude that there is a significant difference between how dealers rate the special features. Inspection of the ratings in the table show that the cumulative score for feature A (95) was the highest score. The brand manager might well be advised to add this feature to the washing machine.

9. Summary. The chapter examines the problem of choosing the correct statistical method to analyse data. Readers are advised to consult Appendix VIII to pursue the statistical analysis in greater depth. Simple illustrations of some of the most commonly applied techniques are illustrated in this chapter.

PROGRESS TEST 12

1. A researcher wishes to establish whether a specific advertising campaign aimed at increasing interest in a new product has been successful. Prior to the campaign, from a sample of 832 respondents, 7 per cent could recall the product's brand name. After the experiment 12 per cent of a further sample of 618 respondents could recall the brand name. Both samples were randomly selected and mutually exclusive. Was the advertising effective in promoting recognition of the brand name? **(5)**

2. Determine whether there is evidence of a relationship between brand awareness and expenditure on advertising in the following example.

Consecutive periods	*Percentage of people aware of the product brand name* ($n = 222$)	*Expenditure on advertising* £'000
1	26.5	91.6
2	31.5	126.4
3	31.5	110.5
4	30.0	112.4
5	29.0	110.9
6	29.5	114.6
7	28.5	107.5
8	28.0	109.6
9	27.5	106.4
10	26.5	103.9

(6)

3. Using the data in problem 2 above, consider what effect a 10 per cent increase in advertising expenditure might have on awareness. **(6)**

4. A marketing researcher is trying to establish whether there is a significant association between a person's marital status and preference for a type of car. The following data is available.

	Car preference			
	Saloon	*Coupé*	*Estate*	*Sports*
Single	61	27	56	106
Married	104	24	107	15
Divorced	92	31	43	84
Widowed	94	42	41	73

Sample size: 1000 respondents.

What conclusion do you think he would reach? (7)

5. A supermarket conducts an experiment to assess whether shelf space or shelf height is more effective in producing sales of tinned asparagus. Three different shelf heights are adopted on consecutive weeks whilst the shelf space is held constant. Three different amounts of shelf space are also used in consecutive three weekly periods. The following results were observed (sales in tins are shown in each cell of the table):

		Shelf space		
		A	B	C
Shelf height	A	24	74	109
	B	31	98	146
	C	32	104	138

What conclusions would you draw? (7)

CHAPTER XIII

The Presentation of Results

1. Introduction. This chapter describes how research results should be written up in report form. Correct report structure is stressed since this will ensure that the results are clearly communicated.

2. Organisation and writing of the research report. Before any report is written, even in draft form, a detailed plan should be prepared. It is appropriate at this stage to decide how the whole report should be organised. A general format for a research report is shown below:

(*a*) title page;
(*b*) table of contents;
(*c*) a brief summary of the research and its results;
(*d*) background to the research;
(*e*) the aims and objectives of the research;
(*f*) the research design;
(*g*) data analysis and results;
(*h*) limitations imposed on the research and its results;
(*i*) conclusions and recommendations;
(*j*) appendixes.

3. Structure of the report.

(*a*) *Title page.* This should specify:
(*i*) date of the report;
(*ii*) names of the researchers;
(*iii*) the topic of the report;
(*iv*) the body for whom the report is prepared;
(*v*) whether or not the report is for limited distribution.

(*b*) *Table of contents.* This should show:
(*i*) a list in order of appearance of all chapters and major sections including subdivisions of chapters or sections;

(*ii*) the appropriate page at which each section commences;

(*iii*) a list of all appendixes;

(*iv*) a list of diagrams and charts preferably on a separate page.

(*c*) *Summary:* a brief outline. This should emphasise the objectives, results, conclusions and recommendations of the research.

(*d*) *Background to the research.* This should portray:

(*i*) a detailed description of the marketing problem;

(*ii*) factors which might influence the problem.

(*e*) *The aims and objectives of the research.* This should consist of a concise statement of the marketing problem and its translation into a research problem.

(*f*) *The research design.* This should not be a major section in the report since most managers have little interest in this aspect. It should contain a summary of the methodology used to meet the objectives of the research report, with a minimal emphasis on techniques.

(*g*) *Data analysis and results.* This should be organised around the objectives of the study and should not comprise a multitude of statistical tables. It should discuss the research findings and summary tables using visual aids to illustrate the points raised in discussion.

(*h*) *Limitations imposed on the research and its results.* Problems encountered and limitations of the research must not be obscured, but should be fully discussed in the report.

(*i*) *Conclusions and recommendations.* A good way to organise this section is to state each objective of the study and then present the specific conclusions relevant to that objective.

(*j*) *Appendixes.* These should be reserved for:

(*i*) items which will appeal to only a few readers;

(*ii*) items which will be required for only occasional reference. These could include sampling methods, detailed statistical tables, interview verification procedure, copies of questionnaires and interview instructions.

4. Detailed approach. Each chapter of a report can be expanded to suit the requirements of the particular study. For example, in a study of the U.K. agricultural tractor market a chapter entitled "Trends in the Industry" may be treated as follows:

Chapter 4 *Trends in the industry*

4.0 General summary.
4.1 A historical perspective of the growth of the market.
4.2 Factors influencing the variations in tractor requirements.
4.3 The current situation: a technical review.
4.4 Current products on the market and the market segments they serve.
4.5 Profiles of each of the major competitors in the market.
4.6 Future prospects for the industry.
4.7 Current and future problems facing the firm.
4.8 Reiteration of the main points.

When a detailed plan of the report structure has been prepared an attempt may be made to write a first draft of the report. It is advisable to think in terms of at least two draft reports before any attempt is made to finalise the report.

5. Additional points to consider when report writing.

(*a*) The reader of the report will probably be less interested in the technical and logical aspects of the research problem than the researcher. Therefore, it is important that the report should stress how the information obtained is relevant to the decision.

(*b*) The report should present the results in an easily understood format, since few managers will have the time or patience to unravel excess verbiage. Red herrings and irrelevancies should be avoided.

(*c*) Managers are seldom versed in research methodology, so there is little point in using terminology which only researchers fully understand. Terms such as skewed distribution, correlation coefficient and even significance level are not necessarily familiar to all marketing managers.

(*d*) It is important to develop an interesting and stimulating style of writing.

(*e*) Visual aids should be used wherever possible, for example, pie charts, bar charts, graphs and relative frequency histograms.

6. Oral presentations of results. These may range from an informal telephone call to a presentation to a large group. In the latter case the use of visual aids is advantageous. The following points should be remembered when reporting orally.

(*a*) Attempt to discover in advance the composition of the audience.

(*b*) Prepare a written script or comprehensive notes.

(*c*) Rehearse the speech timing, especially with respect to technical aids.

(*d*) Employ visual and audio aids wherever possible. Aids include:

(*i*) Chalkboards that allow the presenter to write out and manipulate data as he progresses. Magnetic and felt boards serve a similar purpose.

(*ii*) Flip charts which are large displays arranged on boards in advance of the presentation. These may be used as a static display as well to stimulate informal post-lecture discussion.

(*iii*) Overhead projectors that can present material ranging from one outline to complex overlays. This method projects previously prepared charts drawn on transparent sheets on to a wall or screen. An overlay is produced by the successive additions of new images to the screen superimposed on previous images. The presenter may write on the transparent original during the projection and his amendments will be simultaneously shown on the screen.

(*iv*) Transparent slides. Anything that can be photographed can be projected on to a screen.

(*v*) Tape recordings may be appropriate in some situations but they should be used with care to avoid losing the attention of the audience.

APPENDIX I

A Taxonomy of Statistical Methods of Analysis

(*a*) Where there is a single dependent variable and a single independent variable.

		Independent variable (predictor variable)		
		Nominal scale	*Ordinal scale*	*Interval/ratio scale*
Dependent variable (criterion variable)	*Nominal scale*	Contingency tables and chi square (1,2,3)	Coefficient of differ-entiation (3)	Point biserial correlation coefficient (3)
	Ordinal scale	Coefficient of differentiation (3)	Spearman's rank correlation coefficient (1,3)	Coefficient of point multi-serial correlation (3)
	Interval/ratio scale	Point biserial correlation coefficient (3)	Coefficient of point multi-serial correlation (3)	Pearson product-moment correlation or bivariate regression (1,2,3)

(*b*) Where there are multiple dependent variables and multiple independent variables.

		Independent variable: Nominal scale	Ordinal scale	Interval/ratio scale
Dependent variable	Nominal scale	Cross tabulation and chi square (1,2,3)	Kendall's non-parametric discriminant analysis (4)	Discriminant analysis (1,5)
	Ordinal scale	Analysis of variance (3)	Guttmann – Lingoes CM-2 regression (4)	Carroll's monotonic regression (4)
	Interval/ratio scale	Analysis of variance (3)	Transformed ordinal scales and multiple regression (1,4)	Multiple regression (1,3,4)

(*c*) Where there are multiple dependent variables and multiple independent variables.

		Independent variable: Nominal scale	Ordinal scale	Interval/ratio scale
Dependent variable	Nominal scale	Canonical correlation with dummy variables (1,4)	Dummy variables and transformed ordinal scales with canonical correlation (1,4)	Multiple discriminant analysis (1,4)
	Ordinal scale	Dummy variables and transformed ordinal scales with multivariate analysis of variance (1,4)	As above (1,4)	Transformed ordinal scales with canonical correlations (1,4)
	Interval/ratio scale	Multivariate analysis of variance (1,4)	As above (1,4)	Canonical correlation (1,3,4)

Sources:

1. Nie et alia, *S.P.S.S.* McGraw-Hill, 1975.
2. Harper, W. M., *Statistics.* Macdonald and Evans, 1977.
3. Elliott, K. and Christopher, M., *Research Methods in Marketing*. Holt, Rinehart, Winston, 1973.
4. Green, P. E. and Tull, R. S., *Research for Marketing Decisions.* Prentice Hall, 1973.
5. Wentz, W. B., *Marketing Research: Management and Methods*. Harper and Row, 1972.

APPENDIX II

Methods of Sales Forecasting

1. Methods. A forecast must provide a particular level of accuracy over a specified future time period. Short-run forecasts tend to be more accurate than long-range forecasts. There are three commonly used methods of forecasting:

(*a*) *Judgement methods.*

(*i*) *Aggregate of individual salesmen's forecasts.* Salesmen are asked to make estimates of sales by product to each customer and potential customer over a specific future time period. These are then aggregated (after adjustments for any biases observed in past forecasts) to obtain an over-all sales forecast by product.

Such forecasts are most useful for "next" quarter/month and annual sales forecasts by product. Salesmen base their estimates on available data showing past sales for the appropriate period for each customer.

(*ii*) *Consensus of expert opinion.* A panel of experts (company executives, economists and/or consultants) make individual forecasts from which a consensus is reached through discussion. The method is useful for all kinds of forecasting problems, whether long range or short range. The panel of experts is supplied with whatever data it requests, as far as is possible.

(*iii*) *Delphi method.* A panel of "experts" respond individually to questionnaires that ask for a forecast and the various assumptions that underlie it. The responses are kept anonymous and provided to all forecasters. Successive questionnaires are sent out, and responses are exchanged until a working consensus is obtained. The method is appropriate for annual and long-range forecasts.

(*iv*) *Naïve forecasts.* Such forecasts make use of a very simple "rule of thumb" such as, the next period's sales will be the same as this period's sales, or, next period's sales will be the same as this period's sales adjusted for the change from last period's sales.

(*b*) *Time series analysis and projection.*

(*i*) *Moving averages.* This is a form of statistical forecasting in which the average of the last "n" periods modified in the light of the trend in sales is used to predict the next period's sales. The number of periods, "n", is chosen such that the error in making forecasts is minimised.

EXAMPLE:

Sales of carrots in millions of tonnes

Period	*Sales*	*Three period average*	*Trend difference*
1	2.64	—	—
2	2.72	2.71	—
3	2.78	2.78	+0.07
4	2.84	2.84	+0.06
5	2.91	2.88	+0.04
6	2.88	2.91	+0.03
7	2.93	2.92	+0.01
8	2.96	—	—

The first step is to decide on the number of periods to use as a basis upon which to calculate the moving average. In this case $n = 3$ is chosen arbitrarily just to illustrate the method. Next the average for each set of consecutive three periods is calculated and written opposite the middle period. The trend difference is the difference between one three period average and the next. The formula used to forecast period 9 sales is

$$\text{Latest moving average} + 2 \times \text{trend difference}$$

i.e.

$$2.92 + 2 \times 0.01 = 2.94 \text{ million tonnes}$$

In the case of a four period moving average the trend difference is multiplied by 2.5; for five periods the constant becomes 3; for six periods 3.5 and so on. The general formula to calculate the constant is

$$\frac{\text{number of periods} + 1}{2}$$

Variants of this method include:

Moving totals—in which efforts are made to correct for seasonal factors.

Exponential smoothing—in which greater weight is given to the most recent data in making forecasts.

Interested readers are advised to consult the various texts mentioned in the Bibliography.

Moving averages and associated techniques have the advantage of being simple methods and can be readily used in conjunction with a computer to make short-term forecasts of sales. This is very important where firms have hundreds or thousands of products (or parts, labels and packets) for which to make short-term forecasts.

A disadvantage of moving averages and exponential smoothing is that they both fail to predict upturns or downturns on sales. They cannot show where these changes in direction will occur because they are founded on past data.

(*c*) *Causal methods of forecasting.*

(*i*) *Regression model.* An equation relating sales to predictor variables (disposable income, relative price, level of promotion etc.) is first derived using multiple regression analysis. If forecasts can be obtained independently for the "predictor variables", or sales can be shown to be a "time-lagged function" of one of them, e.g., sales now is a function of last year's earnings, such equations can be used to make good predictions, correctly identifying turning points.

(*ii*) *Surveys of buyers' intentions.* These are used chiefly in connection with consumer durable goods and industrial goods. Customers, potential or actual, are surveyed regarding their intentions to purchase the goods in question during the period ahead. The characteristics of the survey are projected to the size of the universe of customers or potential customers.

(*iii*) *Barometric forecasts.* This takes the form of a time series whose movements precede those of the series to be predicted. For example, a baby food manufacturer has found that the number of births in each area for the previous six months is a good leading indicator of non-milk baby food sales.

APPENDIX III

Cumulative Normal Distribution

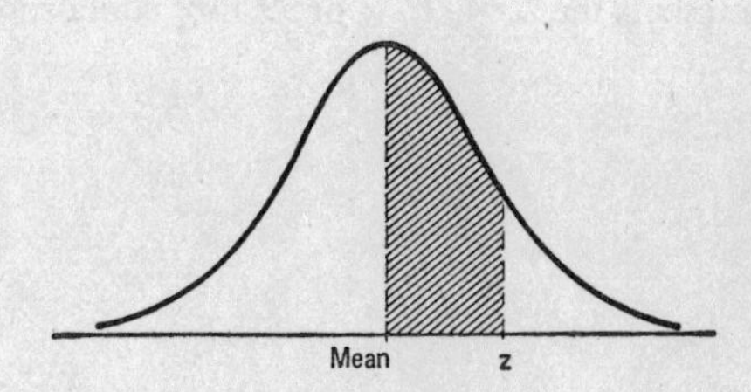

z is the distance the point lies from the mean measured in σs, i.e.

$$z = \frac{Value - Mean}{\sigma}$$

(if z is minus, ignore sign).

z	*Area*	*z*	*Area*
0.0	0.0000	1.6	0.4452
0.1	0.0398	1.7	0.4554
0.2	0.0793	1.8	0.4641
0.3	0.1179	1.9	0.4713
0.4	0.1554	2.0	0.4772
0.5	0.1915	2.1	0.4821
0.6	0.2257	2.2	0.4861
0.7	0.2580	2.3	0.4893
0.8	0.2881	2.4	0.4918
0.9	0.3159	2.5	0.4938
1.0	0.3413	2.6	0.4953
1.1	0.3643	2.7	0.4965
1.2	0.3849	2.8	0.4974
1.3	0.4032	2.9	0.4981
1.4	0.4192	3.0	0.4987
1.5	0.4332		

In estimating a population mean the following z values should be used:

90% confidence level	$z = 1.65$
95% confidence level	$z = 1.96$
99% confidence level	$z = 2.58$

The relationship between "confidence levels" and z values can be observed in the above table. Multiplying the *area* under the curve by z gives the confidence level and the corresponding z value e.g.

$z = 3$ represents the $2 \times 49.87\%$ or 99.74% confidence level.

APPENDIX IV

Selected t and x^2 Values

Degrees of freedom	Level of confidence: t (two-tail) 0.95	t (two-tail) 0.99	x^2 0.95	x^2 0.99
1	12.706	63.657	3.841	6.635
2	4.303	9.925	5.991	9.210
3	3.182	5.841	7.815	11.345
4	2.776	4.604	9.488	13.277
5	2.571	4.032	11.070	15.086
6	2.447	3.707	12.592	16.812
7	2.365	3.499	14.067	18.475
8	2.306	3.355	15.507	20.090
9	2.262	3.250	16.919	21.666
10	2.228	3.169	18.307	23.209
11	2.201	3.106	19.675	24.725
12	2.179	3.055	21.026	26.217
13	2.160	3.012	22.362	27.688
14	2.145	2.977	23.685	29.141
15	2.131	2.947	24.996	30.578
16	2.120	2.921	26.296	32.000
17	2.110	2.898	27.587	33.409
18	2.101	2.878	28.869	34.805
19	2.093	2.861	30.144	36.191
20	2.086	2.845	31.410	37.566
21	2.080	2.831	32.671	38.932
22	2.074	2.819	33.924	40.289
23	2.069	2.807	35.172	41.638
24	2.064	2.797	36.415	42.980
25	2.060	2.787	37.652	44.314

Table continued from page 163

Degrees of freedom	*Level of confidence*			
	t (two-tail)		x^2	
	0.95	0.99	0.95	0.99
26	2.056	2.779	38.885	45.642
27	2.052	2.771	40.113	46.963
28	2.048	2.763	41.337	48.278
29	2.045	2.756	42.557	49.588
30	2.042	2.750	43.773	50.892

EXAMPLE: 5 degrees of freedom, 0.95 level of confidence.

t interpretation: 95 per cent of all sample means of a sample size of 6 (one more than the degrees of freedom) fail within **2.571** standard errors of the population mean.

x^2 interpretation: If x^2 exceeds **11.070** and there are 5 degrees of freedom then one can say with 95 per cent confidence the difference between the actual and the expected results cannot be due solely to chance.

APPENDIX V

F-distribution

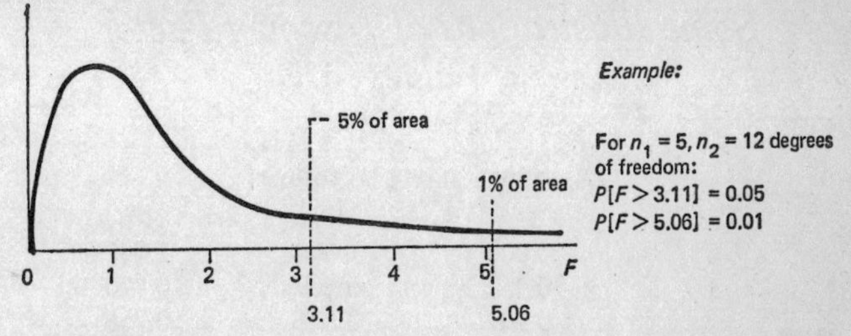

The table below shows selected values for the *F*-distribution. Two levels of significance are shown: the 5 per cent level is shown in roman type and the 1 per cent level is shown in bold type.

n_1 (degrees of freedom for the greater mean square)

n_2 (degrees of freedom for the lesser mean square)	1	5	12	16	20	50
1	161 **4052**	230 **5764**	244 **6106**	246 **6169**	248 **6208**	252 **6302**
5	6.61 **16.26**	5.05 **10.87**	4.68 **9.89**	4.60 **9.68**	4.56 **9.55**	4.44 **9.24**
12	4.75 **9.33**	3.11 **5.06**	2.69 **4.16**	2.60 **3.98**	2.54 **3.86**	2.40 **3.56**
16	4.49 **8.53**	2.85 **4.44**	2.42 **3.55**	2.33 **3.37**	2.28 **3.25**	2.13 **2.96**
20	4.35 **8.10**	2.71 **4.10**	2.28 **3.23**	2.18 **3.05**	2.12 **2.94**	1.96 **2.63**
50	4.03 **7.17**	2.40 **3.41**	1.95 **2.56**	1.85 **2.39**	1.78 **2.26**	1.60 **1.94**

NOTE: Students are recommended to consult a book of statistical tables in order to find the full range of *F* values.

APPENDIX VI

Some Illustrations of Discount Factor Values

	Discount factor percentages		
Year	5%	10%	15%
0	1.000	1.000	1.000
1	0.952	0.909	0.870
2	0.907	0,826	0.756
3	0.863	0.751	0.657
4	0.822	0.683	0.571
5	0.783	0.621	0.497
6	0.746	0.564	0.432
7	0.710	0.513	0.376

General formula:

Discount factor value for any year =

$DFV_{t-1} \times 100/100 +$ Discount factor percentage where DFV_{t-1} is the value of the previous year.

NOTE: Discount factor value in year 0 (i.e. investment time) is always 1.

APPENDIX VII

Answers to Progress Tests

Progress Test 1

1. (*a*) Costs—R. & D. expenditure; introductory advertising and promotion; expenditure on new plant and equipment; production, distribution and administration costs; etc. Benefits—Greater long-term sales and profits etc.

(*b*) Costs—Media placement and design costs. Benefits—Increased awareness of the product; increased interest in the product; etc.

(*c*) Costs—Administrative. Benefits—Better information.

2. (*a*) 4 taking into account probability of occurrence.

(*b*) 3 taking into account probability of occurrence.

(*c*) 3.

Not to take any action.

3. 2.

Progress Test 3

1. (*a*) 3.89 (*b*) 4, (*c*) 4, (*d*) 9 (*e*) 6.10, (*f*) 4.12, (*g*) 2.47, (*h*) 2.03.

2. 3.105 to 6.575.

3. There is no statistically significant difference between the variances.

Progress Test 4

7. 10, 18, 83, 128, 511

Progress Test 12

1. Yes. $Z = 3.169$

2. A strong association exists: $r = 0.80$

3. Awareness will increase by 1.66 per cent

4. That there is a tendency for all "unmarried" people to prefer sports cars; that saloons and estates are preferred by married people; that coupés are preferred by all.

Hint: apply the chi-square statistic.

5. Both shelf height and shelf space are significantly related to sales. Shelf space has the stronger association of the two. Hint: apply analysis of variance.

APPENDIX VIII

Bibliography

Chapter I—Introduction to Marketing Research

Cyert, R. *et alia.* (Ed.), *Readings in Management Decision Making.* Pelican Readings in Management, 1970.

Green, P. E. and Tull, D. S., *Research for Marketing Decisions.* (Ch. 1.) Prentice-Hall, 1975.

Tull, D. S. and Hawkins, D. I., *Marketing Research.* (Ch. 1) Macmillan, 1976.

Chapter II—Problem definition and research design

Skinner, R. N., *Launching New Products in Competitive Markets.* Associated Business Programmes Ltd., London 1974.

Tull, R. S. and Hawkins, D. I., *Marketing Research.* (Ch. 4) Macmillan, 1976.

Wentz, W. B., *Marketing Research: Management and Methods.* (Ch. 2) Harper & Row, 1972.

Wills, G. *et alia.* (Ed.), *Creating and Marketing New Products.* Granada Publishing Ltd., London, 1973.

Chapter III—A quantitative basis for research

Downie, N. M. and Heath, R. N., *Basic Statistical Methods.* Harper International, 1970.

Harper, W. M., *Statistics.* 3rd edition. Macdonald and Evans, 1977.

Yamane, T., *Statistics: An Introductory Analysis.* Harper & Row, 1973.

Chapter IV—Sampling

Chisnall, P. M., *Marketing Research.* McGraw-Hill, 1973.

Kerlinger, F. N., *Foundations of Behavioural Research.* Holt, Reinhart & Winston, 1973.

Wentz, W. B., *Marketing Research: Management and Methods.* (Ch. 8 & 9) Harper & Row, 1972.

Chapter V—Consumer buyer behaviour and marketing research

Chisnall, P. M., *Marketing—a Behavioural Analysis.* (pp. 210–30) McGraw-Hill, 1975.

Fitzroy, P. T., *Analytical Methods for Marketing Management.* (pp. 48–75) McGraw-Hill, 1976.

Giles, G. B., *Marketing.* 2nd edition (pp. 29–38) Macdonald and Evans, 1975.

Mesdag van, M., *British Food Profile.* Halliday Associates, 1978.

Sheth, J. N., Some thoughts on the future of marketing models. *Esomar Conference Main Session,* (pp. 253–61) 1976.

Thompson–Noel, M., Food has changed for good. *The Financial Times.* 5th January (p. 11) 1978.

Chapter VI—Measuring buying attitudes and preferences

Blum, L. M. and Naylor, J. C., *Industrial Psychology: Its Theoretical and Social Foundations.* (pp. 274–305) Harper & Row, 1968.

Chisnall, P. M., *Marketing: a Behavioural Analysis.* (pp. 62–81 and pp. 252–7) McGraw-Hill, 1975.

Green, P. E., Maheshwari, A. and Rao, V. R., Dimensional interpretation and configuration invariance in multidimensional scaling. *Multivariate Behavioural Research.* 4th April 1969.

Green, P. E. and Tull, D. S., *Research for Marketing Decisions.* 3rd edition (pp. 185–90) Prentice-Hall, 1975.

Jahoda, M. and Warren, N. (Ed.), *Attitudes.* (pp. 305–24) Penguin, 1969.

Richards, E. A., A commercial application of Guttman attitude scaling techniques. *Journal of Marketing.* Vol. 22, No. 2. October 1957.

Vernon, P. E., *Personality Assessment: A Critical Survey.* (pp. 279–90) Social science paperback, Tavistock Publications, 1969.

Wentz, W. B., *Marketing Research: Management and Methods.* (pp. 277–94) Harper & Row, 1972.

Chapter VII—Data acquisition—Primary data—Questionnaire construction

Oppenheim, A. N., *Questionnaire Design and Attitude Measurement.* Heinemann, 1968.

Post Office, *A Guide to Effective Direct Mail.* London, 1974.

Rawnsley, A., (Ed.), *Manual of industrial marketing research.* (pp. 26–32) John Wiley & Sons, 1978.

Chapter VIII—Data acquisition—Interviewing

Agrell, T., *Recruitment Techniques.* Thorsons, 1977.

Argyle, M., *The Psychology of Interpersonal Behaviour.* Penguin, 1970.

Aucamp, J., Changes in industrial marketing research. *European Research.* September 1973.

Chisnall, P. M., *Marketing—A Behavioural Analysis.* McGraw-Hill, 1975.

Macfarlane Smith, J., *Interviewing in Market and Social Research.* Routledge, 1972.

. . . 1974 Interviewing techniques. *IMRA Journal.* Vol. 9, No. 2, (pp. 40–52).

Vernon, P. E., *Personality Assessment: A Critical Survey,* Social science paperback, Tavistock Publications, 1969.

Chapter IX—Acquisition of data—experimentation

Tull, D. S. and Hawkins, D. I., *Marketing Research.* Macmillan, 1976.

Chapter X—Data acquisition—Secondary sources within the U.K.

Bird, P., *The Interpretation of Published Accounts.* CAS Occasional paper, No. 14, H.M.S.O., 1974.

C.S.O. 1978, *Government Statistics: A Brief Guide to Sources,* Government statistical service.

Dale, A., *Direct Mail List Building.* The Post Office, 1974.

Rawnsley, A., (Ed.), *Manual of Industrial Marketing Research,* (pp. 9–22). John Wiley & Sons, 1978.

Chapter XI—Data acquisition—Secondary data—sources of international marketing information

British Overseas Trade Board, 1975, *Export Handbook: Services for British Exporters.* 8th edition. London.

B.O.T.B. 1977 *International Directory of Published Market Research.* 2nd edition. In association with Research Finances Management (International) Ltd. London.

Department of Trade & Industry 1971 *Sources of Statistics* (2): *the E.E.C.* London, Statistics & Intelligence Library.

D.T.I. 1971 *Sources of Statistics: E.F.T.A.* London, Statistics & Intelligence Library.

Hellon, J., *Direct Mail and Exporting*. Post Office, 1976.

MacLean, I., Development in official published information in Europe over the next three years. *Cambridge IMRA Conference*, 1977.

Industrial Aids Ltd., *Published Data on European Industrial Markets*. 4th edition. Terminal House, 52 Grosvenor Gardens, London, SW1, 1976.

I.A.A., 1977 *Concise Guide to International Markets*. 3rd edition. Published by arrangement with U.K. Chapter of the International Advertising Association available from L. Stinton & Partners, Kingston upon Thames.

Kline, C. H., *U.S. and Canadian Marketing Surveys and Services*. 2nd edition. Kline & Co., 330 Passaic Avenue, Fairfield, NJ07006, U.S.A., 1977.

Landau, T., (Ed.), *European Directory of Market Research Surveys*. Gower Press, 1975.

Rawnsley, A., (Ed.), *Manual of Industrial Marketing Research*. (pp. 9–22.) John Wiley & Sons, 1978.

Tessler, A., Has export market research a constructive role to play? *Cambridge, I.M.R.A. Conference*, 1977.

Chapter XII—Data analysis

Elliott, K. and Christopher, M. G., *Research Methods in Marketing*. Holt, Rinehart & Winston, 1974.

Green, P. E. and Tull, D. S., *Research for Marketing Decisions*. Prentice-Hall, 1975.

Yamane, T., *Statistics: An Introductory Analysis*. Harper and Row, 1973.

Other References

Nie, Brent and Hull, *S.P.S.S.*, McGraw-Hill, 1975.

APPENDIX IX

Examination Technique

Experience in sitting examinations does not necessarily make one better at passing examinations. Practice in writing examination-type questions and having the opportunity to check out whether the answers are correct is, however, an excellent way of developing examination technique. Progress tests in this book are designed to enable the student to check his ability to retain important facts. Specimen examination questions are given to allow the student the chance to try out actual questions under the guidance of a tutor.

Questions on an examination paper should be scanned in the first instance, with the object in mind of discounting all those questions that the student feels he or she definitely cannot answer or feels ill at ease in answering. The remaining questions should then be carefully studied and the ones which the student feels he or she knows most about, should be tackled.

The time allotted for the examination should be carefully divided up so that an equal amount of time can be spent on each question. Never spend more than the allocated time on a question; it is always possible to return to it later on. If a problem or question involves statistical calculations, remember that it is the methodology and the interpretation of the figures which is most important and that arithmetical accuracy is of secondary importance—though care should be taken to ensure that it is as accurate as is possible.

The following is a suggestion of how to plan one's time in a three hour examination, requiring answers to four questions: First 10 minutes: choose four questions to answer and write brief notes outlining possible ways of answering the questions. Next 160 minutes: spend 40 minutes on each question. Last 10 minutes: read through the script and correct any errors.

APPENDIX X

Specimen Examination Questions

1. What are the most important uses of experimental designs in marketing research? Describe two such designs and suggest marketing situations where these might be applied.

Heriot-Watt University, B.A. (Hons.)

2. "A failure to understand the dynamics of the personal interview can result in the complete loss of the interview." Discuss this statement in the context of an industrial market research interview and outline the special problems that may be encountered by the interviewer.

Heriot-Watt University, B.A. (Hons.)

3. The prediction of future events relies heavily on past experience. How might a firm predict future sales of:

(*a*) existing products;

(*b*) new products.

Illustrate your answer by reference to a consumer durable firm.

Heriot-Watt University, B.A. (Ordinary)

4. Of what value has the product life cycle concept been to marketing researchers? Illustrate your answer with examples.

Heriot-Watt University, B.A. (Hons.)

5. What are the main types of observational technique used in marketing research? Illustrate your answer with examples.

Heriot-Watt University, B.A. (Hons.)

6. Indicate the major sources of information to which manufacturers of consumer durables may refer in order to formulate marketing strategies.

Heriot-Watt University, B.A. (Ordinary)

7. What is meant by the "projective" method of acquiring behavioural data? Give examples of the main types of projective techniques used by researchers.

Heriot-Watt University, B.A.) (Hons.)

8. "Advertising is only one of several marketing forces acting upon potential customers and moving them towards buying action." Examine the implications of this statement for adver-

tising effectiveness research and suggest, with examples from industrial and consumer markets, how advertising goals might differ from marketing goals.

Heriot-Watt University, B.A. (Hons.)

9. Decisions can only be as good as the information upon which they are taken. How can a marketing executive try to ensure that he always has the best information available at all times?

Heriot-Watt University, B.A. (Ordinary)

10. How would you justify the use of quantitative models in marketing in the light of current behavioural theories of the firm?

Heriot-Watt University, B.A. (Hons.)

11. What are the essential differences, if any, between industrial and consumer marketing research? In what ways has the scope of Industrial Marketing Research widened in the 1970s?

Heriot-Watt University, B.A. (Hons.)

12. You are employed in the Marketing services department of a U.K. based manufacturer of fork lift trucks. The company is considering entry to the Middle East markets and you are asked to prepare a quick preliminary report on its prospects. What information would you try to assemble for this purpose and where and how would you obtain it?

Heriot-Watt University, B.A. (Hons.)

13. Although researchers are clearly concerned with purchasing behaviour, they appear to spend a great deal of time attempting to measure consumers' perceptions and attitudes. Why should this be? Outline the main methods of measurement.

Heriot-Watt University, B.A. (Hons.)

14. What is the main objective of experimentation in marketing? Describe three experimental designs and suggest marketing situations where these might be applied.

Heriot-Watt University, B.A. (Hons.)

15. "The existence of an adequate sampling frame is a critical factor in a survey's success." Elaborate on this statement. Describe critically the main sampling frame used: (*a*) in a general household survey; and (*b*) in an industrial products survey.

Heriot-Watt University, B.A. (Hons.)

16. Few firms have modelled the marketing process in mathematical terms. Why should this be so?

Heriot-Watt University, B.A. (Hons.)

17. Technological forecasting would seem to be the domain of

the engineer/scientist. Should marketing analysts become engaged in this activity?

Heriot-Watt University, B.A. (Hons.)

18. Is industrial marketing so different from consumer marketing as to require separate approaches to researching buyer behaviour? What particular problems does the analyst face in researching industrial buying behaviour?

Heriot-Watt University, B.A. (Hons.)

19. The hotel company to which you are marketing adviser is considering building an addition to its chain in southern Spain, close to Gibraltar. What research would you undertake before giving your opinion on the feasibility of the project?

Institute of Marketing, Diploma

20. Discuss, with examples, the merits and disadvantages of conducting marketing research by means of:

(*i*) mailed questionnaires;
(*ii*) retail panels; and
(*iii*) consumer panels.

Institute of Marketing, Diploma

21. When questionnaires are compiled, it is important that these are pilot tested. Explain what this entails and what it should bring to light.

Institute of Marketing, Diploma

22. As Marketing Director of a watch and clock manufacturing company what research would you institute before advising whether the company should manufacture digital wristwatches?

Institute of Marketing, Diploma

23. It has been said that 20 properly conducted depth interviews yield more information then a general survey of 2,000. Comment.

Institute of Marketing, Diploma

24. Briefly describe the merits of quota and random sample selection, explaining why the former is generally used by industry and the latter more often by government in surveys.

Institute of Marketing, Diploma

25. List some of the major points to be kept in mind if a questionnaire is to be fully effective and explain their importance.

Institute of Marketing, Diploma

26. Discuss the theoretical basis governing the size of samples used for market research and describe how these are effected by the needs arising from their use in practice.

Institute of Marketing, Diploma

27. What is the importance of socio-economic groups in present day market research?

Institute of Marketing, Diploma

28. Your company is concerned with the provision of wine-making kits for the home. What research methods would you undertake in order to advise the company regarding the optimum pricing and packaging strategies to adopt in this market?

Institute of Marketing, Diploma

29. There are many potential sources of error where personal interviews are employed for research purposes. List some of these and indicate means by which their effects can be minimised.

Institute of Marketing, Diploma

30. Describe the services a market research agency provides for its clients. When should a company use its own research resources in addition to using agency services?

Institute of Marketing, Diploma

31. Discuss the principles to be taken into account in drawing up a sample of light engineering establishments.

Institute of Marketing, Diploma

32. A company employs several hundred merchandising salesmen who endeavour to ensure that its products are adequately displayed and shelves in supermarkets fully stocked. Each is allocated a group of about 50 outlets, including a number under the same management, and located in a defined area.

The Sales Director wonders whether restriction to 25 outlets with nearly double calling frequency would not improve overall sales: the smaller outlet would not then receive merchandising visits. The salesmen do not normally take orders for products. Discuss the problems in setting up an experiment to help this decision. Sketch a possible solution.

Strathclyde University, B.A.

33. A random survey of 88 users of public houses showed the following responses for frequency of eating meals in public houses for socio-economic groups as follows:

	ABC1	C2	DE
once a week	17	6	6
once a month	17	4	11
once a year	5	1	8
never	3	4	6

Is there any association between these two classifications significant at the 10 per cent level? Explain the assumptions required for the test you use, and the particular advantage of this test.

Strathclyde University, B.A.

34. Omega Research Ltd., specialise in consultancy, design and execution of research for firms engaged in the supply of financial services of all types to the public. Omega management believe they have unusual skills in:

1. Selecting samples of respondents representative of different types of investor and buyers of financial services such as insurance, tax consultancy and investment counselling.
2. Developing and administering structured questionnaires to elicit details of personal financial behaviour and circumstances which respondents may be ordinarily reluctant to discuss.

However, Omega believes its business to be expanding more slowly than that of its competitors. It sees these competitors as being more skilled in gaining publicity and attracting new business. Omega is uncertain whether these various competitors have a different price policy from its own (which is to charge very modest prices) and indeed how important price policy is. Omega has consulted a research consultant to help make an objective enquiry.

Develop proposals for such an enquiry to be conducted to help Omega write a marketing plan for the next three years. Among other things, enumerate question headings or areas of interest for the enquiry; do not compose any detailed questionnaire, even if you consider one would be necessary. Make and state whatever assumptions you consider reasonable about the structure of the financial service industry.

Strathclyde University, B.A.

35. "Research studies differ considerably but virtually all marketing research is approachable through a more or less common set of procedures . . . which provide operational guidelines."

Identify and comment upon the major stages of such a set of procedures.

Preston Polytechnic H.N.D. Business Studies

36. What do you understand by the term "sample frame"? What criteria might you use to evaluate a frame?

Preston Polytechnic H.N.D. Business Studies

37. Discuss the steps you would take in setting up a test market operation for any consumer good of your choice.

Preston Polytechnic H.N.D. Business Studies

THE USE OF CASE STUDIES IN EXAMINATIONS

Sometimes examining bodies set case studies in lieu of formal examination questions. Unfortunately it is not possible to show case studies in a book of this nature and merely showing questions relating to case studies would of course be meaningless. A number of points should be borne in mind when trying to prepare for an examination which requires answers to be given to specific questions about a case study. These are as follows:

1. Questions set will expect candidates to demonstrate what they know about the subject of marketing research. Knowledge of marketing theory and business in general will be assumed.
2. It is highly likely that one of the questions set will test for a general knowledge of the purpose of marketing research and the specific kinds of information that it can provide to management. A comprehensive knowledge of research methodology will be expected.
3. The case study may pinpoint a particular problem which requires a solution to be found. One should not overlook, however, the fact that there may be even broader issues to be researched.
4. It will be important to be able to relate the costs and benefits of marketing research to the problem highlighted in the case study. This should be reflected in any research design which is suggested.

Since case studies are usually made available to students some time before the actual examination (often up to a month) and there is thus opportunity for students to obtain advice from other people, it is unlikely that the question asked in the examination can easily be predicted. Often further information is introduced at the time of the examination. There may be a number of possible correct answers—but a "correct" answer to a case study is one which shows an ability to analyse a situation in a logical manner and to recommend a course of action which will go some way to suggesting a solution. In the case of a marketing research case study, the solution must reflect knowledge of research methodology as well as a correct diagnosis of the problem situation.

Index